THE BEST ADULT JOKE BOOK EVER

THE BEST ADULT JOKE BOOK EVER

JOHNNY SHARPE

INDEX

First published in Great Britain by
Arcturus Publishing Limited
First Floor
1-7 Shand Street
London
SE1 2ES

for Index Books
Henson Way
Kettering
Northants
NN16 8PX

This edition published 2000

Printed and bound by
WS Bookwell in Finland

Cover Illustration by Jim Hansen
Cover Design by Communique
Text Design by Zeta @ Moo
Edited by Emma Hayley

© Arcturus Publishing Limited

ISBN 1 84193 030 X

CONTENTS

MEET MAN'S BEST FRIEND

A man took his dog to the vets and asked for its tail to be completely removed.

"But why?" asked the vet "that's a bit drastic."

The man replied

"My mother-in-law's coming to stay next week and I want to make sure there are no signs of any welcome."

★ ★ ★

The dog auditioned for a part in the new summer show. He told half a dozen jokes, using different accents, tap-danced and closed with a song.

"What d'you think?" the owner asked the agent.

"Well, I don't know," replied the agent, shaking his head. "The delivery's good but the material is weak."

★ ★ ★

As the stranger walked into the store, he saw a sign that read "Beware of the Dog". The next moment he saw an old sheep dog sprawled out on the floor, fast asleep.

"Is that the dog referred to on that sign?" he asked the storekeeper.

"Yes, it sure is," came the reply.

"Well, it's hard to believe the dog is so dangerous. Why did you put the sign up?"

"Because since I've put the sign up, they've stopped tripping over him."

★ ★ ★

After fifteen years of service in the house of Lord and Lady Muck, the cook was asked to leave to make way for someone younger and more dynamic. On the day of departure, she received her final wages, only to discover that the stingy pair had thrown in a meagre £10 extra as a 'thank you' for loyal service.

"Well, I never!" she exclaimed, throwing the money at the dog.

"Why on earth did you do that?" they demanded.

"At least I'll show proper appreciation to those who've worked hard. That's to say thanks to the dog for helping me clean all the dishes over these past fifteen years."

★ ★ ★

The woman went along to the dog behavioural centre to tell them about her problem pet.

"He keeps chasing cars," she explained.

"Well, not to worry. It's quite normal and in time the dog will grow out of it."

"But you don't understand," she wailed.

"He keeps burying them in the back garden."

★ ★ ★

The man was very proud of his guard dog, which he would leave outside his house to warn off any would-be burglars. Then one day, there came a frantic knocking at the door and on opening it, the man saw a distressed woman.

"Is that your dog outside?" she cried.

"Yes," he replied.

"Well, I think my dog's just killed it."

"What!?" roared the man. "What sort of a dog have you got?"

"A peke."

"A peke!" he exclaimed. "How could your dog kill my big guard dog?"

"I think it got stuck in his throat," she replied sadly.

★ ★ ★

"Hey, come over here," hissed a voice. Looking round the man could see no one but an old mangy greyhound.

"Yes, over here," said the greyhound. "Look at the state of me. I'm stuck here in this shed when I should be out winning more races. I was a triple champion in my time, you know."

The man was dumbfounded. A talking dog! He could become famous. Everyone would want to see it. Millions could be made. He went to look for the dog's owner.

"I'd like to buy your dog," he said, "is it for sale?"

The owner shook his head and said

"No mate, you don't want that old thing."

"Oh but I do," persisted the man. "I'll give you £100 for it."

"Well all right, but I think you're making a great mistake."

"Why's that?"

The dog's a bloody liar. He's never won a race in his life."

★ ★ ★

The baker's shop was quite empty when the dog walked in with a basket in his mouth, a list and money tied round his neck. The assistant looked at the list, filled the basket with two loaves of bread, three doughnuts and a treacle tart, and the dog left swiftly. Every Tuesday afternoon the same thing would happen. The dog would arrive at the quietest time, get the basket filled and then disappear. The assistant became more and more intrigued. One Tuesday, she decided to follow the dog and discover where it went when it left the shop. Having got permission for some time off, she closely followed the animal. He crossed the busy high street, took a short cut up an alley, walked across the park and strolled into the council estate. Five minutes later, he turned into a garden and walked up to the front door where he rang the bell.

All of a sudden, the door was flung open and the dog was booted back down the path. Outraged at this behaviour, the assistant called from the road.

"What do you think you're doing? This is a very special dog, don't treat it in such a cruel way."

"Get lost," snarled the man. "This bloody dog's got to learn. That's the second time this month he has forgotten his keys."

★ ★ ★

A woman went to the pet shop to sell her dog.

"I only want £10 for him," she said. "I just want to get rid of him."

The pet shop owner began shaking his head so the dog immediately interrupted.

"Oh please buy me," he said, "otherwise, she'll do away with me. I've been as good a pet as possible. I ran all the errands for her, mowed the lawn – but the trouble was, she couldn't stand me beating her at chess all the time."

The pet shop owner was astonished.

"Goodness, a talking dog!" he exclaimed. "Why are you selling him for just £10, you could get a lot more."

"I want rid of him quickly," she replied. "I'm fed up with his lies."

★ ★ ★

A man tried to smuggle a puppy into the country to avoid the quarantine laws, but accidentally drew attention to himself as he tried to walk casually through customs. He had put the dog down his trousers but every time he took a step, his whole body would shake and he kept making little moaning sounds. "Excuse me sir, is there anything wrong?" enquired the customs official.

"Yes Officer," gasped the man in a strangled voice. "I tried to smuggle a puppy into the country by putting it down my trousers."

The officer smiled knowingly. "And, of course, you've now come a cropper because it's not house trained."

"Oh it's not that," replied the agitated man, "I've just discovered it's not weaned."

★ ★ ★

The dog breeder was advised that if she wanted a 'champion', some of the dog's hair needed to be removed from its underside. She went along to the chemist and asked for some hair remover.

"This is the most efficient product," said the chemist, showing her a small tube of cream, "but it's advisable to keep your arms up in the air for at least two minutes before taking it off."

"Oh no, you misunderstand me," said the woman, blushing. "It's for my Chihuahua."

"Oh I see," he replied, "that's no problem, just don't ride a bike for a couple of hours afterwards."

★ ★ ★

"I'm sorry Doreen," said her husband gently. "Old Rover's getting very old, he can hardly walk and he doesn't hear so well anymore. I think you have to prepare yourself for the worst."

"Nonsense," replied his wife, "there's nothing wrong, look I'll show you."

"Come on Rover," she called. "Come here Rover, and sit."
"Oh dear," sighed her husband. "I told you his hearing was
affected. I'll go and get the mop and bucket."

★ ★ ★

A man and his dog go into a bar and order two pints of beer.
"I'm sorry," says the barman, "but no dogs allowed in here."
"Why not?" asks the dog. "I'm not going to cause trouble."
The barman is dumbfounded.
"Bloody hell!" he exclaims, "a talking dog. This is fantastic.
Have a drink on me."
A pleasant hour passes and then the man disappears to the loo.
Seeing the dog on his own, the bartender asks him if he would
pop into the bakery down the road and give his mate a shock by
asking him for a loaf of bread. The dog agrees and the bartender
gives him £5 for the purchase.
A moment later, the man returns from the loo and panics when
he sees the dog is missing.
"It's all right mate, he's just gone down the road for me."
But it's not all right! The man has never allowed the dog out on
his own before so he chases after him. As he passes an alleyway
he hears strange sounds coming from it and walking down it, he
finds his dog humping a white poodle.
"Hey Gruff," he shouts. "What the hell's going on? You've never
acted like this before."
"I know," says the dog, "but you see, I've never had £5 before."

★ ★ ★

A gorilla has escaped from the local zoo and taken refuge at the top of a tree in a neighbouring garden. The householder rings the zookeeper who arrives 10 minutes later with a pair of handcuffs, a Doberman pincher, a stick and a shotgun.

"Okay," says the zookeeper to the man. "I'm going to go up after him and poke him with this sharp stick. When he falls to the ground, the dog will go for his balls and as the gorilla puts his paws over them to protect himself, you slip on the handcuffs."

"That sounds easy enough," replies the man, "but what's the shotgun for?"

"Now listen carefully, this is most important. If I fall out of the tree before the gorilla, shoot the fucking dog!"

★ ★ ★

"Just give me a shandy," said Bob to the landlord.

"Blimey, you must be bad," replied the landlord, shaking his head. "I've never known you to order anything less than a double scotch."

"No. I'm on the wagon," replied Bob sadly. "I got so drunk last night, I went home and blew chunks."

"Oh come on!" said the landlord. "Everyone does that now and again."

"No, no, you don't understand," groaned Bob. "Chunks is the name of my dog."

★ ★ ★

Why do dogs stick their snouts in blonde's crotches?
Because they can.

★ ★ ★

A man walked into a country pub with a flea bitten old dog on a lead. The bar was full of wise old country folk, most of them had big dogs lying at their feet. He addressed the crowd.

"See here," he said, pointing to his dog. "This dog understands everything I say. Not just command words like "sit", "lie", "beg" and all that crap, but proper sentences. I'll wager anyone £2 that he'll do exactly as I say."

The customers looked down at the mangy old dog and one by one they look up the bet until there was nearly £100 in the kitty.

"Okay," said the man, putting up his £100. "Watch this". He picked up his dog and threw him on the open fire. "Patch, get off that fire!" he yelled.

★ ★ ★

Before the race meeting had begun, some of the horses were boasting about their achievements.

"Well I've won over half the races I've been in, and I've been placed in the rest," said the bay horse.

"I've won 18 races out of 24," said the black.

"I've only lost one race in the whole of my career," said the white.

"Excuse me," interrupted a greyhound who'd been listening to them, "I've won 20 races out of 20."

The horses looked down on him in astonishment.
"Bloody hell," said one, "a talking dog!"

★ ★ ★

A woman was walking through the park when she spotted a man and a dog playing chess. She watched the game for a few minutes and then remarked,

"I can hardly believe what I'm seeing. A dog playing chess. What a clever animal!"

"He's not that clever, madam," replied the man. "I've beaten him four games out of six."

★ ★ ★

MEET MR ANGRY

A difficult customer complained that there was a hair in his venison stew.

"I don't expect to find this in a top class hotel," he said angrily, "so I'm not paying for it."

Later, the waiter met the man again when he was asked to take up room service. This time, he found the man with his head between a young woman's legs.

"Aah," said the waiter, still angry from their earlier confrontation. "I see you don't mind hair in your mouth now."

"No, I don't," retorted the man. "But if I find any venison stew down here, I won't pay for this either."

★ ★ ★

The man had had a bad day and it got no better when he sat down in the restaurant for his lunch. He ordered the roast chicken and as it arrived, he was just about to tuck in when the head waiter rushed over to his table.

"I'm so sorry," said the waiter, clearly agitated. "There has been some terrible mistake. There is only one portion left and this was meant for the man over there." He pointed to a gorilla of a man sitting in the corner looking very angry.

"Well tough," said the man, still in a bad mood. "It's here now and I'm going to enjoy it."

Again he picked up his knife just as the gorilla walked up to his table.

"Listen punk," he snarled, "that's my chicken, touch that and you're dead. Whatever you do to that chicken, I'll do to you. Cut off one of its legs and I'll cut yours off, pull off one of its wings and I'll pull off one of your arms."

The man hesitated a moment and then slowly stuck his finger up the bird's backside, pulled it out and licked it.

★ ★ ★

Each day the world famous celebrity would greet the crowd before entering his hotel. One of his adoring fans was John Lovitt who arrived early on the first two days so that he could stand at the front. But both times the celebrity had passed him by and walked further down the line to an old bedraggled tramp, and whispered something in his ear. John was so keen to get the same attention that he searched out the tramp afterwards and offered him money for his old clothes. On the third day, he stood there wearing the tramps clothes and sure enough the celebrity made a bee-line towards him. Putting his hands on John's shoulders he whispered

"I've already warned you twice you filthy bastard, next time I'll get my men on to you. Now fuck off and don't come back!"

★ ★ ★

"Waiter," called the angry customer. "Is this crab fresh?"
"Of course, sir," replied the waiter, adding confidently, "it

walked up from the beach this morning."
"Well in that case," said the customer scornfully as he sniffed it with distaste "it must have stood in something on the way."

★ ★ ★

A man goes to the supermarket to buy some tins of cat food but is told he cannot buy them unless the cat is with him. The following day he returns to buy some hamster food but again he is refused.

"I'm sorry sir, the rules state that you can only buy pet food if you can prove the reason for buying it."

The man storms out extremely angry but returns the next day with a small bag. He asks the cashier to put her hand in it, which she does.

"Mmm, what is it?" she muses, "it feels soft and squidgy."

The man replies smugly, "Now if you're satisfied, I'll have this packet of toilet rolls."

★ ★ ★

A man is sitting quietly in the café having a cup of tea when an old tramp comes and sits beside him. After a few minutes, there's the most awful smell and putting his hand over his nose, the man turns angrily to the tramp and says,

"You dirty bastard, have you crapped yourself?"

"I have," replied the tramp.

"Then get out of here and go and do something about it."

"I can't, not yet," came the reply. "I haven't finished."

19

★ ★ ★

"I want to open a new bank account, NOW!" yelled the nasty customer.

"Of course, sir," replied the teller, "but there's no need to shout."

"Just open the bloody account," he replied.

"Okay, just one moment."

"NOW!" he shouted, "get off your fat arse and get on with it."

Upset at the language, the bank teller walked off and returned with the manager.

"For fuck's sake, I want to open a bank account, I've just won £20 million on the lottery," he said.

"Immediately, sir," replied the manager and he turned to the teller, saying

"Get your fucking arse into gear and open an account."

★ ★ ★

"I can't sleep in that room," said the angry man to the receptionist. "It stinks in there."

"I'm sorry sir," she replied, "the last occupant had a skunk with him. Perhaps if you opened the windows..."

"What?" he interrupted, "and lose all my pigeons!"

★ ★ ★

A woman had bought a parrot for her children but it wasn't until she got it home that she realised he had the most obscene language. She banned it to the back bedroom, away from the little toddlers, and tried hard to get it to change its ways. But to no avail. Every time she walked in, it would screech at the top of its voice

"Hello, you fucking tart, how about a good shag?"

One morning, she was in the house on her own and brought the parrot down to the kitchen while she was baking.

"Come on Duke," she would say, "here's a piece of fruit, say thank you."

"Bugger off," came the reply.

All of a sudden, she'd had enough. She didn't want to listen to him a moment longer, so she shoved him in the freezer to cool off. He squawked loudly for a minute and then went very quiet.

"Oh no," she thought, "what have I done and immediately opened the freezer door.

Out walked the parrot, looking very prim and proper.

"Good morning, madam," he said. "I must apologise for my bad behaviour, I hope we can start afresh."

The woman was delighted. She put him back in his cage and took him into the front room.

"By the way," he said a moment later, "what did the turkey do?"

★ ★ ★

A motorist pulled up beside a man tending flower boxes in a pretty little Cotswold village.

"I just had to stop to congratulate you on the marvellous display of flowers," he said.

"At least someone appreciates it," replied the man gruffly. "I look after all the flowers in the village, but do they thank me?

Do they call me John the horticulturist? No! And look," he said, pointing to the church. "Look at all the repairs to the intricate stonework. But are they pleased? Do they call me John the stonemason? No! And yet, and yet..." he said, going red in the face with anger. "Just one sheep, just one bloody sheep!"

★ ★ ★

MEET THE ADULTERER

"What the hell's going on here," screamed the husband, as he walked unexpectedly into the bedroom and found his wife in bed with another man.

"I'll beat your bloody brain's out," he yelled.

"Now, now," said the wife. "Just listen a moment. You remember I told you I'd won the lottery? Well it wasn't quite as you think. George, here, is my winning ticket (pointing to her lover). He's paid off the mortgage for us, bought our new car and even arranged our holiday to the Seychelles."

"Okay, okay," said the husband, calming down, "the least you can do is cover him up properly. It's quite chilly out there today."

★ ★ ★

But I can't believe it!" exclaimed her husband, "pregnant? How can that be? I've always been so careful."

"Now, now," she said comforting him. "What makes you think it's your fault?"

★ ★ ★

"I guarantee sir," said the pushy salesman, "that this machine will give you the answer to anything you want to know".

"Mmm," mused the company director, "we'll see." He thought

for a moment and asked. "Where's my father?"

"He's in the Dog & Duck on Fetter Street, drinking his third pint of lager," said the machine.

"Ah ha," said the director triumphantly, "it's wrong. My father died two years ago."

The salesman looked astonished. "But it's never wrong," he blustered. "Let me try."

"Where is Mr Pettigrew Senior, this gentleman's father?"

The machine replied immediately.

"Mr Pettigrew senior died two years ago and is buried in South Heighton Cemetery. But this man's father is down the Dog & Duck, just ordering his fourth pint."

★ ★ ★

A man came home early from work to find his wife in bed. Immediately suspicious, he looked under the bed and then opened the wardrobe door to find a naked man standing amongst the clothes, waving his hands in the air.

"What the hell's going on?" screamed the husband.

The lover quickly replied "I'm from 'Bugs are History Ltd' and I'm here about the dreadful infestation of moths."

"What moths?" snapped the husband, "and where are your clothes?"

The lover looked down in astonishment and replied "Those little bastards, it's much worse than I thought."

★ ★ ★

A woman was determined to impress her husband's business associates by inviting them to a lavish dinner party. Early in the morning on the day of the do, she instructed her husband to visit the high class deli on the high street and pick up some live snails – that way they'd be fresh until the last minute. Cursing under his breath, Eric set off for the shop but on the way he noticed his sexy-looking neighbour, beckoning to him.

"Hello Eric," she cooed, standing there in a skimpy negligee. "I'm so scared of ladders, would you be a dear and change the light bulb in the hall for me."

A little overawed by her presence, Eric changed the bulb, stopped for a cup of tea and before he had time to realise what was happening, found himself upstairs giving her his all. Time after time, they romped between the sheets until they both fell asleep exhausted. Suddenly, Eric sat bolt upright, looked at the clock and realised he only had 15 minutes to get to the shop before it closed. He rushed out and got there just in time, bought the snails and hurried home. However, in his haste, he caught his finger in the garden gate and with a cry of agony, dropped the snails all over the path.

"Where the hell have you been?" bellowed his wife from the bedroom window.

Eric looked at his wife's snarling face, then he looked down at the snails and said

"Come on boys, we're nearly home."

★ ★ ★

Knowing her husband wouldn't be home till late, the woman brought her lover back to the house for some frolics.

"Hold on, I can't," her lover said suddenly, "I've forgotten to bring the condoms."

"Oh that's all right, my husband's got some."

But after searching for them for five minutes, she returned angrily to the bedroom.

"The bugger's taken them with him, I knew he didn't trust me."

★ ★ ★

A man was in bed with his mistress when he heard his wife arrive home early.

"Quick," he whispered, "get over in the corner."

As she stood there, he covered her in talcum powder, draped a silk scarf around her private parts and told her to act like a statue.

"And what's that?" asked his wife casually, as she walked into the room.

"Just a statue darling," he replied. "It's nice, isn't it – a bit like the one in our neighbour's bedroom."

Later that night, once the man had fallen asleep, his wife disappeared downstairs and returned with a cup of tea. She walked over to the statue and hissed

"Here, take this, I bet you're feeling thirsty, I certainly was, stuck all that time in our neighbour's bedroom!"

★ ★ ★

The poor woman was so neglected by her husband that she decided to buy a pet to keep her company. As she walked round the shop, she suddenly saw a poor old parrot, stuck away in the corner of the shop in a dusty old cage. The parrot had lost his feet so nobody wanted to buy him. The poor woman's heart went out to the little bird and she walked over to his cage.

"Hello, old thing," she said. "You look a bit lonely."

"I am," he replied. "I like talking to people. I've got a lot of interesting things to say, but no one's interested because I haven't got any feet."

"But how do you hang on to the perch?" she asked.

"With my dick," he replied.

It only took the woman a moment to decide that the parrot was exactly what she wanted, so she paid for him and they went home. Over the next few months, they would spend hours in deep conversation, and the woman was so happy, she hardly noticed her husband's neglect any more. Then, one afternoon, she arrived back from the shops to be greeted by a very serious bird.

"I've got something bad to tell you," he said. "While you were out, your husband came home with his secretary. They sat on the sofa, kissed and cuddled, then he took her blouse off and started to fondle her breasts."

"Oh no!" she cried. "What happened next?"

"I don't know," he screeched. "I fell off my perch."

★ ★ ★

The man's wife was in labour, and he rushed her into the new maternity unit where he was asked if he would take part in a special experiment. He was told that they had perfected a way to transfer some of the labour pains to the husband, so that both partners could share the experience. He readily agreed and they began. Some hours went past and because the husband felt well, more pain was transferred over to him, until he took it all and left the wife to have the baby with complete ease. The following day, they took the baby home to find the gasman dead on the doorstep.

★ ★ ★

Alfred was extremely suspicious of his wife's sudden enthusiasm for golf, so he hired a private detective to follow her and see what was going on.
A few days later, the private detective reported back.
"It would seem that your wife spends a great deal of time in the rough with one of the young golf instructors," he said.
"Oh no," wailed Alfred, his head in his hands, "how long do you think this has been going on?"
"Well sir, considering the number of freckles he has on his backside, certainly for the last month during this hot spell of weather."

★ ★ ★

A man was going away on business for a month. Highly suspicious that his wife would get up to no good while he was gone, he hired a private investigator to follow her wherever she went. On his return, the P.I. confronted him with his wife's infidelity. All the evidence was on video. The man was shown film of his wife at glamorous parties, dancing the night away at exclusive nightclubs, intimate dinners with one of his work colleagues, overnight stays at luxury hotels...

"Well," gasped the man, "I can hardly believe it."

"Is it because she's involved with one of your colleagues?" asked the P.I.

"No, no," replied the man. "I just didn't believe my wife could be that much fun."

★ ★ ★

Lady Sylvia became very suspicious of her husband, when every morning at 4 o'clock he would get up and disappear downstairs saying he was going to check the boundaries of their estate, after reports of strangers in the area. Lady Sylvia was convinced her husband was having an affair with their pretty maidservant, so she devised a scheme to catch him out.

Unbeknown to her husband, she gave her maidservant the weekend off to spend with her relatives. That night when he got up again at 4 o'clock and went downstairs, she quickly jumped up and ran down the back way to the maid's bedroom. Quick as a flash, she jumped into the maid's bed, and it wasn't long before she heard the window being opened

and a shadowy figure come into the room. Determined not to say anything but surprise him afterwards, she submitted to his lovemaking.

Afterwards, she spoke. "So you'll be off to check if there are any suspicious people about."

"Not likely," came the reply. "The master and his wife want the gardens looking their best for the May Day celebrations on Monday."

★ ★ ★

Two old friends were talking over a pint of beer.

"I must say," said Malcolm. "You're the Catholic, you're not allowed to use birth control and yet you have only two children and I, who can use anything, have five kids. I don't understand."

"Oh, it's quite simple really," replied John. "We use the safe period."

"What's that then?"

"Every other Tuesday, when you play darts."

★ ★ ★

Connie was devastated. Today she'd discovered her husband was having an affair with their next-door neighbour.

"But why George? What's she got that I haven't. You could hardly call her god's gift to women."

Tired of all her questions, he decided to be brutal, but honest. "The thing is, Connie, she's different in bed. You just lay there like a sack of potatoes, but she moves around and moans a lot. It really turns me on!"

That night, Connie was determined to put on a good show. She wore her sexiest negligee (not seen since the honeymoon) and five minutes into his thrusting she started to move about and moan, "George, it's been an awful week. First the milkman got our monthly bill wrong, then the car ran out of petrol, I think I'm going down with a bad cold..."

★ ★ ★

Gerald was feeling guilty. He'd had a dreadful argument with his wife before leaving for work, and he'd said some unforgivable things. Not least that she was no bloody good in bed. He decided to ring her up and apologise.

It took ages for her to answer the phone, in fact, he was just about to ring off when he heard her say "hello?"

"Oh June, it's me," he said. "Where were you?"

"I was in bed," she replied.

"In bed!" he exclaimed, "in the middle of the day! Why?"

She thought for a moment and replied "I was just getting a second opinion."

★ ★ ★

Every Saturday morning, without fail, Derek would get up at 6 o'clock to go down to his allotment. If the weather was bad, he'd potter about in the greenhouse. However, this particular Saturday there'd been a bad car accident and the road had been closed, so he was unable to get there. He returned home and decided to surprise his wife with a cup of tea. As he entered the bedroom, he whispered lovingly "Here you are darling, a nice refreshing cup of tea. It's a lovely morning, the sun's really quite hot."

His wife, still half asleep, mumbled from beneath the duvet. "Is it? I expect Derek will be down there by now getting sunburnt, knowing him!"

★ ★ ★

An artist and his sexy model were canoodling in the conservatory when they heard her husband's car drive up.

"Quick," whispered the artist. "Take your clothes off so it looks like we're working."

★ ★ ★

A mafia boss arrives home early from work and discovers his wife in bed with one of his bodyguards.

"You no good motherfucker," he bawls. "I'm going to shoot your bollocks off."

"Oh give us a chance, give us a chance," pleads the bodyguard frantically.

"Okay," says the boss, "swing 'em."

★ ★ ★

A woman decided to buy herself a pet because she saw so little of her family and was becoming very lonely. Unfortunately, the pet shop owner had just sold the last puppy and had promised the kittens to a little girl who was coming to collect them later in the day.

"All we've got left is this parrot," said the shop keeper. "He's a good talker, but he used to live in a sleazy nightclub and casino, so his language can be a bit colourful."

But the woman was desperate for company so she bought the bird and took it home. That night her husband arrived home late, followed closely by her two teenage girls.

"Look what I've bought," she said triumphantly, pulling the cover off the cage. As they all peered in to see the surprise, the parrot opened his eye and remarked

"Well, bugger me! Different place, different madam, better-looking girls but the same old clients. Hello Tommy!"

★　★　★

How can a wife tell if her husband is being unfaithful?
She gets it pretty soft.

★　★　★

A man arrives home early from work and catches his wife in bed with another man.

"What the hell's going on here," he yells, "who's this?"

"Mmmm, that's a good question," she replies. "Hey, lover, what's your name?"

★ ★ ★

Bob's wife was convinced her husband was having an affair so she decided to spy on him. That Saturday, they were invited to a fancy dress party but she pretended she had a headache and urged him to go on his own. Then, 30 minutes later, she put on a costume that hid her face and went to the party to see what he got up to. Just as she thought, every time he spoke to a girl, he put his arms round her shoulders and whispered sweet nothings in her ear. To test out her theory of unfaithfulness, she then made a play for him herself and in less than 20 minutes, they'd found a spare room and were writhing around on the floor. Shortly afterwards, she left and the next morning she prepared herself for the confrontation.

"How did you like the party?" she casually asked.

"Rubbish," he replied. "Not my sort of thing at all. I only stopped a few minutes, lent my costume to that prat Alan Taylor, and went down the pub to play darts."

★ ★ ★

The angry woman marched into the hairdresser's and confronted a woman who was having a perm.

"You old tart!" she yelled. "Thought you wouldn't get found

out, messing with my husband!? Well, I've got the proof and I'll show it to you."

She opened her handbag and pulled out three photographs.

"Here, take a look at this. There's one of you and my husband sharing a table in the White Hart. See, there's another showing him with his arm around you and then there's this one where you're kissing and I don't know what he's doing with his hand. So what do you say to that then?"

For a few moments, the woman looked at the photographs. Then she replied

"Mmm, not bad, I'll have one each of the first two and two copies of the third."

★ ★ ★

The couple had enjoyed a passionate afternoon in bed. Now as they lay there half-asleep, they hear the sound of a car pulling up outside.

"Quick, quick," she urges, "it's my husband, you'd better get out of here."

The man jumps up and heads straight for the window. He's just about to jump out when he stops dead and says angrily "Hold on a minute, what's going on? I am your husband."

★ ★ ★

The man stormed out of the cinema demanding to see the manager.

"How dare you let such filth go on in your cinema. Look over there. A couple on the back row have been fondling each other all the way through the film and now she's taken out his todger and is stroking it."

"Calm down sir," said the manager, hoping no one will see the fuss.

"To be honest, sir, they're nowhere near you and they aren't bothering any of my other customers. Just forget about it and enjoy the film."

"I can't," cried the man. "That woman is my wife."

★ ★ ★

The man's meeting was cancelled so he rang home to surprise his wife. The maid answered.

"Can I speak to my wife please," he said. There was a moment of silence before the maid replied

"I'm sorry sir, she's not available at the moment."

The husband was immediately suspicious.

"Where is she?" he demanded, "and don't lie or you'll lose your job."

"In bed, sir."

"Is she alone?"

"No sir."

"Is she with a man?"

"Yes, sir."

The husband was overcome with uncontrollable anger.

"Now listen to me," he said. "Get my hunting rifle from the study, go upstairs and shoot the buggers dead. Hurry, I'll hang on till you return."

He waited with his ear to the phone and heard two gunshots, then a few moments later the maid came back on the line.

"It is done, sir."

"Good girl. Now drag the bodies out to the summer house and leave them there until I get home."

"But sir," she protested, "we don't have a summer house."

There was a pause before the man asked apprehensively, "Is that Baymouth 443987?"

★ ★ ★

MEET THE BEST MATE

Two men become firm friends when they found themselves in the same hospital ward. Both had had their tongues removed through a serious illness and when they were better, they decided to go out on the town and pick up a couple of girls to celebrate their recovery. After a few drinks, they found two girls and by a series of graphic hand signs, managed to get them to agree to go for a ride with them. As they parked up in Lovers' Lane, one of the men signalled to the other,

"Have you got any condoms?"

"No," signalled the other. "You'd better get down the all-night chemist and buy some."

He handed the man a £10 note and off he went.

Five minutes later, the man returned and made signs explaining that the chemist couldn't understand him.

"That's easy," signed the other. "Just get your dick out and put it on the counter. He'll understand."

Another two minutes went by and the man returned crestfallen.

"What happened?" they asked.

The man signalled, "I did what you suggested. I put my dick on the counter and showed him my £10. He then put his dick on the counter. It was bigger than mine, so he pocketed the money."

★ ★ ★

A man went to the doctor about his best friend.

"It's Bob, doctor, he's been told to give up smoking because of his bad health, but he just can't seem to do it. Have you got any ideas, I'd really like to try and help him."

The doctor thought for a moment and then said "Yes, I've got an idea that could cure him. Before he smokes his packet of cigarettes, stick each one up your arse first, without him knowing, and then put them back in the pack. That should do the trick."

And indeed it did. After a week had gone by, the man's friend told him he'd definitely given up fags because they left a foul taste in the mouth.

Pleased with his success, the man happened to bump into the doctor the following day in the street. He told him the good news but then continued "The trouble is doctor, how do I stop this dreadful need to stick cigarettes up my bum?"

★ ★ ★

"How did you get on at the doctor's, Pete?" asked his old mate, George.

"Well, he thinks he can do something for me," replied Pete. "He's told me to drink a glass of this medicine after a hot bath."

"So do you feel any different?"

"Not yet, I've only managed to drink half the bath water up to now."

★ ★ ★

Two best mates are out drinking when they spot a girl standing at the bar all alone.

"Watch this," says Dave, and he saunters over, gets chatting to her and they eventually leave arm in arm.

The next night, the two men are there again and who should walk in but the same girl, on her own.

"Hey, look," says Dave, "there's that little raver. Go on Bill, chance your arm, she'll soon have your trousers down."

So Bill goes over, gets chatting and not long after, they leave together.

The next day they meet up at work and compare notes.

"What d'you think?" asked Dave.

"Not bad," replied Bill, "but she's not as good as my wife."

"Yeah, I agree," nodded Dave. "She's not as good as your wife."

★ ★ ★

"I'm fed up, Steve," sighed his mate, Jack. "Bloody sex, it's a minefield. If you go out with girls you might get something rotten like herpes. If you go out with boys, you get AIDS. In fact, you can't even go out with yourself anymore for fear of getting repetitive strain injury."

★ ★ ★

"You know Fred, I gave up booze and sex once," said Jack.

"Never, I don't believe you," came the reply.

"It's true. It was the worst 40 minutes of my life."

★ ★ ★

"I'm getting a divorce," said Jack to his mate, Bill. "The wife hasn't spoken to me for six months."

Bill thought about this for a moment and then replied, "Just make sure you know what you're doing, Jack. Wives like that are hard to find."

★ ★ ★

"Cor Steve, you look dreadful, what's wrong?"

"It's this bloody toothache. It's driving me mad. I just don't know what to do."

"Well, I've got a cure," said his mate. "When I had a toothache a couple of months back, my wife gave me a blow job and the pain disappeared just like that," he said, clicking his fingers.

"Well, thanks for that," said Steve. "Will your wife be in tomorrow."

★ ★ ★

"Oh my throat's so sore," said Doreen to her friend.

"Well do what I do and suck on a life saver," she replied.

"That's easy for you to say, but I don't live near the coast like you."

★ ★ ★

Two mates are in the urinals and when John sees the size of Kevin's penis, he remarks jealously

"Bloody hell Kevin, you've got quite a trophy there. Puts mine to shame."

"Oh, it's not so hard to get one like this," he replies. "All I do is knock it on the wardrobe door four times each night before I go to bed."

So, remembering Kevin's words, John strips off that night and knocks his penis against the wardrobe door four times. On hearing this, his wife turns over half awake and says "Is that you Kevin."

★ ★ ★

"If I don't do something soon, our marriage is down the Swanee," said Bill to his mate.

"What is it then? The eternal triangle?"

"Yeah," he nodded sadly.

"Listen Bill, I had that problem once but we managed to get back on track."

"Yeah? How come?"

"We ate the sheep."

★ ★ ★

Two men talking over a pint of beer.

"Me and the wife had a terrible argument last night," said Alf. "She's a bloody stubborn woman. But I got the last word in."

"Good for you, Alf," said his mate, "and what was that?"

"Okay, buy the damned thing," he replied.

★ ★ ★

Two girls – one out for a good time, the other more staid and religious – go out clubbing for the night. Julie thoroughly enjoys herself, but Monica is not at all happy. As the club closes, they are approached by two boys who offer to walk them home. It's not long before the boys make their move – arms round the shoulders and a little nibbling of the girls' ears.

"Oh no!" gasps Monica, "dear Lord, please forgive them for they know not what they do."

"Leave it out," hisses Julie, "mine does."

★ ★ ★

"Jack sat quietly nursing his pint of beer."

"Hello mate," said Bob, coming to sit beside him, "you're quiet tonight, anything wrong?"

"It's me and Angie," he replied, "our sex life is so boring, sometimes I wonder why we got married in the first place."

"Come on, cheer up," replied Bob. "I think I've got the answer. You just need to spice it up a bit. Catch her unawares, that often does the trick."

When Bob saw Jack a couple of weeks later, he looked much happier.

"So it worked then?" asked Bob.

"You bet," smiled Jack. "The following afternoon I bought her a big bunch of roses and a box of chocolates, rushed into the house, grabbed her from behind, pulled down her knickers and did it there and then on the living room carpet."

He paused, then added

"Mind you, I don't know what the vicar thought, he was taking tea with her at the time."

★ ★ ★

Saturday morning at the library, Martin spots Kevin over in the non-fiction section.

"Hello Kevin, been away? Haven't seen you for a while."

"Oh hello, Martin. As a matter of fact I have. I went on a weekend course to that big hotel off the A1. It was all about reincarnation. Very good. Mind, it cost £400."

"Phew! That's a bit steep."

"Yes, I suppose it was. Still, you only live once."

★ ★ ★

"How did your date go last night?" Tracy asked her friend.

"Strewth! he wouldn't stop talking, so I had to sit on his face in the end," came the reply.

★ ★ ★

Two girls were chatting on the top deck of a bus.

"Oh Beryl, I had such a funny experience on the way home from work the other night. There was only me and this gorgeous looking bloke in the carriage and we'd not long left the station when he came and sat down right beside me. Well! Before I knew what was happening, he started kissing me and then he put his hand up my jumper and began playing with my nipples. Mmm..."

she said, thinking back. "Anyway, after a bit he got his willy out and asked me to hold it while he put his hand up my skirt..."

"Yes, and then what?" asked Beryl impatiently, "what happened next?"

"Now hold on," said her mate, "I'm not that kind of girl. I pressed the emergency button, didn't I?"

★ ★ ★

Bob looked sadly into his beer and shook his head in bewilderment.

"Women!" he said, "I'll never understand them."

"What's wrong?" asked his mate. "It was last week," began Bob, "I'd had a couple of pints, felt a bit randy so I went round Julie's place and had some sex. Well twice, actually. Then I felt thirsty, went and had another couple of pints and felt this urge on me again. So I popped back to Julie's and we did it again, three times.

"Well that really did give me a thirst so back round the pub I went and had four pints. It was early evening then, so I walked back to Julie's, we had two bottles of wine and we jumped back into bed. Then I got a bit worried about missing last orders so I rushed back round to the pub and got in another four pints. What I didn't know was that there was a late extension, so I supped three more pints and staggered back to Julie's at one. Trouble is, I just couldn't get it up and do you know what she said?"

"Are you seeing other women Bob?"

* * *

"Your hair's looking good these days," commented Charlie to his work mate.

"Yeah," he winked. "I get my girlfriend to strip and rub my hair between her tits. This is the result. You ought to try it."

"Yeah, I think I will."

They met up at work a couple of days later and Charlie asked how it went.

"Great!" he said. "It really worked. By the way, you've got a lovely house."

* * *

"Oh Patsy, you know that gorgeous man across the road, he was banging on my door for almost an hour last night."

"Well, why didn't you open it?"

"I didn't want to let him out."

* * *

"That bloody Billy Parkes. He put his hand up my skirt last night so I slapped him across the face. Wish I hadn't."

"Why? Did you really hurt him?"

"No. He was chewing tobacco at the time."

* * *

Jack turned to his mate and said

"The doctor reckons my depression will go away if I bring a bit more excitement into my marriage. He says when he feels low, he goes home, has the wife on the dining room carpet, takes her out to dinner, stops in at a nightclub then goes home for a night of erotic passion. He says it works for him."

"So are you going to do it?"

"Yeah, I'm going round to his wife's at 7.30pm."

★ ★ ★

"Where's Joe tonight?" asked his mate, sipping his second pint of beer.

"He's not able to come in," replied the landlord, "his wife's broke a leg."

"Well that shouldn't stop him," came the reply.

"It was his leg she broke."

★ ★ ★

"Max, you look dreadful, what's happened?" asked his mate.

"My girlfriend's father told me I could marry his daughter if I could tell him what 6+3 equalled. Luckily I had my wits about me and said ten."

"Phew!! That was close."

"But that's the trouble. He said it was close enough."

★ ★ ★

MEET THE BOOZER

The man walked into the bar, clothes torn, scratches down his face and a big black eye.

"What happened to you?" asked his mates.

"I was fighting for Joan Clark's honour," he replied.

"Really?!"

"Yeah, but she wouldn't give it up."

★ ★ ★

The man staggered into the bar and shouted

"A double whisky bartender, and a drink for all your customers... and have one yourself."

"Well, thank you sir."

Moments later, the man shouted again

"Let's have another drink all round and one for yourself, bartender."

"Excuse me sir, but I think you ought to pay for the other round first."

"But I haven't got any money."

The bartender was beside himself with rage.

"Then fuck off out of here and don't ever come back," he roared.

However, ten minutes later, the man reappeared, and once more staggered to the bar.

"Double whisky," he slurred, "and a drink for all my friends."

"I suppose you'll be offering me a drink as well," growled the bartender sarcastically.

"Oh no," replied the man, "you get nasty when you drink."

★ ★ ★

"Gerald," said his wife angrily. "What time do you call this? You went down the take-away three hours ago and now you have the nerve to stagger back in here, stinking of booze. What about me?!"

He replied "How does a chicken tikka, vegetable madras, pilau rice and two chapattis grab you?"

"Lovely," she replied.

"Okay," he said, and threw up all over her.

★ ★ ★

The man stormed into the bar and yelled

"Okay you bastards, which prat just painted the back of my car pink?"

From the corner, a huge 6'5" gorilla of a man stood up and growled

"I did. You got a problem with that?"

"No, no," stuttered the man. "I just thought you'd like to know, the first coat is dry."

★ ★ ★

The judge said to the drunk

"Please stand, Mr Havermore. Before passing sentence, I need to know if you are sober enough to understand you have been brought here for drinking."

"Oh, that's very kind, your Honour, but I won't if you don't mind. I couldn't touch another drop."

★ ★ ★

A man walked into a pub with a big grizzly bear on a lead, and asked for a pint.

"What's your game, mister?" asked the landlord. "You can't come in here with that," he said, pointing to the bear, "get him out of here."

"Oh come on, mate, he's not doing any harm," pleaded the man. "Anyway, there's something very special about him."

"Oh yeah," said the landlord scornfully, "and what's that then?"

The man beckoned the landlord closer and said

"This bear will give you the best blow job ever. I guarantee it."

"Bollocks," replied the landlord.

"No, I swear to you, it'll be the best you've ever had. Go on, give it a go. Just hit him on top of the head with a stick."

So, out of curiosity, the landlord agreed. He hit the animal's head with a stick and the bear went round the other side of the bar and gave the landlord the best blow job in the world.

"Wow," gasped the landlord afterwards. "Anyone else want to try it," he said to the other customers in the pub.

A little old lady appeared through the crowd and replied "I'll have a go, but don't hit me too hard with the stick."

★ ★ ★

An Englishman, an Irishman and a Scotsman walked into a bar and each ordered a pint of beer. However, when the drinks arrived, all three pints had a fly swimming around in the froth. The Englishman looked at it disgustedly and pushed it away. The Irishman picked his out with his fingers, threw the fly on the floor and then drank the beer. The Scotsman also picked his fly out of the froth, then began shaking it over the top of the pint, saying "Come on you bugger, spit it out, spit it out."

★ ★ ★

Three Englishmen are looking for a fight. As they walk into their seventh pub of the night, they spot an Irishman sitting in the corner.

"Hey, watch this," says the first Englishman winking. He goes up to the Irishman and speaks.

"I hear St Patrick was a shirt-lifter."

"Is that so," replies the Irishman sipping his beer.

Unable to get an angry reaction, the second man goes over and adds

"I hear S. Patrick was a shirt-lifter and a pervert."

"Is that so now?" comes the reply.

"I've got it lads," says the third Englishman. "Listen to this."

He walks over to the Irishman and growls "I hear St Patrick was an Englishman."

The Irishman looks up at him and replies "Yes, that's what your mates have been telling me."

★ ★ ★

A drunk staggers into a bar and spots a man drinking in the corner. He goes up to him and says at the top of his voice.

"I've just shagged your mum, it was great."

There's a hushed silence as everyone waits to see a reaction, but the man ignores the comment and the drunk wanders away. But 10 minutes later he shouts at him again from the other end of the bar.

"And I'll tell you now, your mum's the best lay for miles."

Again, everyone waits with baited breath but nothing happens. They all return to their drinks but by now the drunk can't leave it alone. He staggers over to the man once more and yells

"And another thing, she says she wants it from me every night."

Sighing audibly, the man puts down his beer and places his hand on the drunk's shoulder.

"Just go home dad, you've had enough."

★ ★ ★

A man walks into a pub and sees a girl on her own at the bar. He beckons the landlord over and tells him he wants to buy her a drink.

"I wouldn't bother, mate," replies the landlord. "She's a lesbian."

"That doesn't matter," he says. "I'd still like to buy her a drink."

A moment later the girl receives her drink, looks over at the man, smiles and says thanks. Taking that as a sign of approval, he swaggers over to her and begins "So whereabouts in Lesbia do you live..."

★ ★ ★

The old drunk staggers down the road and walks into an exclusive shoe shop instead of the brothel on the other side of the road.

"I want some service," he bellows, so the manager puts him in a side room where he won't annoy the other customers.

"Someone will be along in a minute," he tells the drunk.

While he's waiting, the drunk gets out his dick and puts it on the table.

"Aah!" exclaimed the shop assistance coming in, "that's not a foot!"

"I know, I know," he retorts. "Just a little more time and it soon will be."

★ ★ ★

Two old men had drunk a pint together, every day for over 20 years. Sadly, one day Tom died, and Albert was left on his own. The last words that Tom had ever uttered were

"Albert, me old buddy, in memory of me, have an extra pint each day."

Albert kept his promise and each day he ordered an extra drink. Then one day, to the amazement of the bar staff, he only had one drink.

"What's happened Albert, no drink for your friend?"

"Oh yes, I've just had the pint for Tom, I always promised him that, but I've had to stop. The doctor's told me my liver's packing up."

★ ★ ★

"If you don't keep the noise down, I'm going to have to arrest you," advised the policeman to the drunk who was staggering down the road singing at the top of his voice.

"Oh, have a heart officer," slurred the man "it's the works' outing."

The policeman looked round him, "where are the others then?"

"There aren't any others," he replied. "I work for myself."

★ ★ ★

Two drunks missed the last bus home so ended up trying to walk. But as they reached open countryside, one of them sank to his knees in the middle of the road and refused to go any further. He laid down, closed his eyes and was soon fast asleep. The other drunk eyed his mate in astonishment.

"You silly bugger, you'll end up like a squashed hedgehog,"

he remarked as he settled himself on the grass verge and fell asleep as well. Just after midnight, a car came down the road and seeing the man lying in the middle of the road, he swerved suddenly and ended up on the grass verge!

★ ★ ★

A drunk sets out to go fishing. He gets his tackle box, rods and net, and staggers off to look for a likely spot. Soon, he comes across a huge area of ice and starts to saw a hole. All of a sudden a booming voice speaks from nowhere. "There are no fish under that ice."

The drunk looks round but can't see anyone so he continues to saw. Again the voice booms

"I've told you once, there are no fish under that ice. You're wasting your time."

The drunk looks up, there's still no sign of anyone so he continues sawing.

"That's enough!" shouts the voice. "Pick up your gear and get out of here, or there'll be trouble"

"Where are you?" yells the drunk. "If you're a ghost trying to scare me, then bugger off."

"No," replies the voice. "I'm the manager of this bloody ice rink."

★ ★ ★

A man rushes into a bar and orders six glasses of single malt whisky. As the landlord puts each one down on the counter, the man picks it up and downs it in one.

"Why the hurry?" asks the landlord.

"It's all to do with what I've got in my pocket," he replies.

"Really," says the puzzled landlord. "What's that?"

"Just 75p."

★ ★ ★

A man walks into a pub and is greeted by a crocodile.

"What'll it be?" he asks.

The man just stares at him open-mouthed.

"Come on," he says, "haven't you seen a crocodile before?"

"Oh sorry," he stutters, "it's just that I never thought the horse would sell this place."

★ ★ ★

Martin walked into the pub with both arms bandaged, a black eye and badly bruised hands.

"What happened to you?" asked his mates.

"Too much to drink last night," he answered ruefully. "I remember staggering out of here, next thing I know, I'm going up Station Road, straight across the middle of the roundabout and down that steep bank by the side of the railway line. Bloody awful, it was. It's a good thing I didn't have the car with me."

★ ★ ★

Jack was having a dreadful time with his drinking. It had got to the point where he was spending more time in the pub than at work, and he was in grave danger of losing his job.

"Willpower," he said to himself. "I must have more willpower." As he approached the pub, he decided to test his willpower out, and walk straight by. And he did it! One hundred yards past the door, he heartily congratulated himself. "Well done Jack, you did it. I knew you could, and I think that calls for a celebration. Let's go and have a drink."

★ ★ ★

A man goes on a three-day bender, and during his drunken spree he falls over, gives himself a black eye and damages his best suit, ripping off all the buttons and completely pulling out the right-hand pocket of his trousers. When he sobers up, he looks at the state of himself, and then his clothes with alarm, afraid he's lost all his personal effects.

He reaches inside his jacket pockets and happily his keys and wallet are still there. Then he tries his trousers. He puts his hand in the left-hand pocket and brings out some small change. Then he puts his hand in the right-hand pocket, feels around and mumbles to himself, "How come I ended up with a couple of prunes?"

★ ★ ★

"What's that?" asked the man, sitting next to a drunk at the bar.
"I don't know," replied the drunk, "It's a bit rubbery, but it could be plastic."
"Mmm..." mused the man, "let me have a look." He rolled the object between his fingers and then handed it back.
"So where did you get it from?"
"My nose," came the reply.

★ ★ ★

A man and a giraffe walk into a bar and both have a pint of beer. Then they have another pint and this continues until they are very drunk. The man gets up to leave and staggers to the door. The giraffe tries to follow but collapses on the floor in a dead faint.
"Hey!" shouts the barman to the man. "You can't leave that lying there."
"It's not a lion, it's a giraffe," he replies.

★ ★ ★

"Your usual, Ken?" asked the barman.
"No, not tonight, thanks," replied Ken sadly. "My wife's told me that if I go home one more time so drunk that I've puked all over myself, then she'll leave me."
"Excuse me," said a man sitting next to him, "I couldn't help but hear what you were saying and I think I've got the answer. Make sure you've got a £10 note handy. Then when you get home,

legless and probably covered in vomit, tell her someone else puked up on you. Show her the £10 note and tell her he offered to pay to have your suit dry cleaned."

Ken cheered up immediately and ordered the first of many pints. By the time he staggered home, he was very drunk and, true to form, had puked up all over himself.

"Why, you disgusting little man," roared his wife, "you've done it again."

"No, no, my dear," said her husband soothingly. "I didn't do this. Someone else was sick all over me. Look they gave me £10 to get the suit dry cleaned."

"But that's not £10, that's a £20 note," she said.

"Oh yes .... er .... that's because he also shat in my pants."

★ ★ ★

The man was absolutely legless by the time he left the pub. He staggered out, barely able to see, and headed home on automatic pilot. But on the way, he had a silly idea. He decided to take a short cut across the old factory site. He stumbled over the rubble, fell over more times than he could remember and then climbed over a wall which was topped with broken glass. On this, he badly cut his backside but he continued on his way and eventually made it home. The pain on his backside pierced his drunken haze so when he'd crept upstairs, he went into the bathroom to survey the damage in the mirror. He dabbed it with cotton wool, put some plasters on and went to bed.

"Well, well, well," said his wife the next morning, banging down the tea tray and making him wince. "You really were drunk weren't you?"

"I don't know what you mean," he replied lamely. "I only had a couple."

"Bullshit," she replied. "I know you were very drunk and I'll tell you why. When I went into the bathroom this morning, the mirror was covered in plasters."

★ ★ ★

"I'm arresting you for being drunk," said the officer.

"But how can you tell?" he asked.

"You're walking along with one foot on the pavement and one foot in the gutter."

"Oh thank you officer, thank you very much," he replied. "For a moment, I thought I had one leg shorter than the other."

★ ★ ★

A man walks into a pub, orders a pint of beer and drinks it down in one go. Then he pees all over the floor.

"You disgusting bugger," cries the landlord, "that's the last pint you have here."

The poor man is very embarrassed, he stutters his apology so sincerely that eventually the landlord gives him a second chance and pulls him another pint. The man drinks it and pees all over the floor again.

"Right, that's it," bellows the landlord seeing red, "get out and never come back. You're barred."

Three months go by and the man returns.

"Get out," yells the landlord, and the man whimpers and rushes away. Then, one lunch-time, a few months later, the landlord is surprised to see him come in again.

"I thought I told you not to come back," he says.

It's all right landlord," says the man confidently, "I've been to a psychiatrist and he tells me I have a nervous complaint. It's all sorted now."

The landlord sees the man has changed so he allows him to stay and pulls him a pint of beer.

Woosh! He drinks the pint and pees all down his leg onto the newly fitted carpet.

The landlord is beside himself with rage. He can hardly believe it.

"You fucking prat, you told me it was all sorted," he said.

"Yes, it is," smiles the man. "I've been to the psychiatrist and he's cured me of my embarrassment. He's taught me to feel good about myself!"

★ ★ ★

As the drunk staggered out of the pub, a fire engine went hurtling by, the bells clanging wildly. Immediately, the drunk gave chase but after a minute or two he collapsed on the street puffing loudly.

"Oh fuck you!" he shouted, "if that's the way you want it, you can keep your bloody ice creams!"

★ ★ ★

"It's bloody odd," said Jack to his mate. "Whenever I get drunk, some bugger comes into my bedroom when I'm asleep, pees in the wardrobe and pukes in my shoes."

★ ★ ★

"A pint of less please landlord," said the customer.
"I'm sorry sir, I don't seem to have any. Is it a spirit?"
"I don't know," came the reply. "My doctor suggested it. When I went to see him this morning, he suggested I drink less."

★ ★ ★

Gavin has had a really heavy night in the pub and when he staggers home at two in the morning, he falls into a deep sleep as soon as his head touches the pillow. Unfortunately, he wakes up two hours later to discover he has wet the bed. So being a real toss-pot, he climbs over his wife onto the dry side and rolls her into the wet. Moments later, she wakes up ranting and raving about who has wet the bed.
"You know it wasn't me," she yells. "And I can prove it." She gets out the potty, sits on it and pees long and satisfyingly.
"Okay, I'll show you," he responds and takes his turn on the potty. It's a struggle at first but eventually he also has a long pee...
A minute later he wakes up to find he's wet the other side of the bed as well."

★ ★ ★

Drinking at the bar, a man is repulsed when a huge fat ugly woman comes and sits down next to him. Ignoring her completely, they both continue to drink for another hour and then she speaks.

"Phew, if I have any more to drink, I'm really going to feel it."

He replies "Do you know, if I have another drink, I probably won't mind."

★ ★ ★

MEET THE CASTAWAY

A man had been stranded on a desert island for two years when he experienced severe shaking of the ground and noticed a great tidal wave bearing down upon him.

"Oh Lord, please help me," he prayed. Suddenly, a boat appeared and a man aboard shouted to him urgently.

"Quick, get on board, before the tidal wave comes."

"No, no, I have faith in Jesus," said the castaway. A few moments passed and another boat appeared.

"Quick man, don't be silly, get on board, there's not much time left."

But again he replied

"No thank you, I have faith in Jesus."

With only seconds to go, another boat appeared and a voice called out in panic

"If you don't get over here right this minute, it'll be too late."

"No thank you. I have faith in Jesus."

The next moment, the tidal wave hit the island, smashing everything to pieces. The poor castaway drowned.

Later in heaven the man met Jesus and said reproachfully

"I had faith in you. I can't believe this has happened."

"What do you mean, you can't believe it. I sent three bloody boats to save you!" cried Jesus.

★ ★ ★

A man and his dog got stranded on a desert island, and as time went on, they ran out of food and things looked pretty grim.

"I'm sorry Yap," said the man, "one of us has got to eat," and with that he killed the dog and put him in the cooking pot.

For three days, he dined well, until there was nothing left of Yap but a pile of bones. The man looked at them sadly and said to himself, "It's a pity old Yap isn't here. He'd have loved those bones."

★ ★ ★

A man had been stranded on a desert island for three years. As he gazed out to sea one day, he suddenly started jumping up and down in excitement and talking to himself.

"Oh wow, oh wow, there's a boat coming, and on the boat is a beautiful naked girl beckoning to me, swivelling her hips..."

As he spoke, his erection got bigger and bigger and suddenly he grabbed it with two hands.

"Fooled you, fooled you," he screamed, "there ain't no bloody boat."

★ ★ ★

MEET THE CLERGY

The man was in a great deal of trouble. He'd just lost a fortune on the stock market and it looked as if it was going to affect his business. After a sleepless night, he got up early and went down to the parish church. He knelt before the altar and prayed fervently.

"Oh dear God, please let me win the lottery on Saturday."

But it was no good. The following week the situation worsened. A vote of no confidence was passed by his board and he was forced out of his own company. Again, he went to church.

"Oh please, dear God, let me win the lottery this week."

But still he had no luck. Penniless and out of work, his wife left him and his house was repossessed. He sat down in the front pew and prayed frantically.

"Oh dear God, I've lost everything. Please, oh please, let me win the lottery. Why won't you let me win?"

Suddenly, the church trembled and lights flashed. Then God's voice boomed out

"You silly, silly man. You could have at least bought a lottery ticket and given yourself a sporting chance."

★　★　★

The local vicar was looking for some of the older children to help him out at Sunday school. He spotted Matthew sauntering down the road and asked him if he could have a quick word. Wondering what was going on, Matthew followed the vicar into church and sat down in one of the pews. The vicar was eager to know how much Matthew knew about church so the first question he asked was
"Where is God?"
Matthew stared at him in astonishment, but didn't say a word.
"Come on Matthew," he said again, more forcibly, "Where is God?"
Terrified, Matthew jumped up, ran out of the church and raced home, locking himself in the bedroom.
"Hey Matt," called his elder brother. "What's all the rush? Are you all right?"
"No, I'm not," sobbed Matthew. "I'm in real trouble this time. God's gone missing and the vicar thinks I did it."

★ ★ ★

Thousands of pounds worth of repairs were needed to make the old church tower safe. But funds were low and it would take the small congregation a lifetime to raise such a great amount of money. It so happened that the village was home to a multi-millionaire who would take up residency two months every year and make the odd appearance at church. The vicar decided to approach the man and invited him down to see for himself the bad state of the building. As the millionaire walked round the outside of the tower, a piece of crumbling stonework fell off and hit him on the head.

"Ouch," he cried, rubbing his head.

"I see what you mean, vicar, it does need something doing. Here, take this cheque for £100. As the man turned away to go back to his car, the vicar turned his eyes heavenward and cried

"Go on, dear Lord, hit the old skinflint again."

★ ★ ★

A man came home from church with a bloody nose.

"Good gracious!" exclaimed the wife. "You've only been to church, what happened?"

"It was old Mrs Biggins that did that," he complained. "I was only trying to help. She was sitting in front of me and when we got up to sing, her dress had got caught in the cheeks of her bum. So I pulled it out. Whack, she was so bloody nasty about it."

The following Sunday, he came home with a black eye.

"Oh, I don't believe it," said the wife. "Don't tell me it was Mrs Biggins again."

He nodded sadly. "That's the last time I try and help," he said angrily. When we got up to sing, the dress was caught in the cheeks of her bum again and this time the man next to me pulled it out. Now I know she didn't like that so I put it back... And this is all the thanks I get."

★ ★ ★

The party was in full flow when the priest knocked at the door.

"Oh come in Father," said the hostess, holding a large glass of whisky. "Come and join the fun. I'm sure you don't mind a few adult games," she said winking at him coyly. "In fact, I think you'll like this one. The men are all behind a sheet which has just one hole cut out. Each of them in turn sticks their willy through and the women have to guess whose it is. It's great fun. Do come and join us."

The priest looked shocked.

"My goodness! I can't condone such behaviour," he exclaimed.

"Well I don't see why not. Your name has come up at least four times," she replied haughtily.

★ ★ ★

What did the clergyman call a double orgasm?
The second coming.

★ ★ ★

A devout churchgoer and her 16-year-old daughter attended church every Sunday without fail. On this particular Sunday, the vicar was waiting to greet his parishioners as they left church and happened to notice a slight bulge on the daughter's stomach.

"Good morning Mrs Dogood," he said smiling, "it looks as if your daughter is putting on a little weight."

The woman blushed with discomfort.

"Oh, nothing to worry about," she replied, "just a little wind."

A few months later, the vicar noticed the girl had got even larger.
"Are you sure everything's all right?" he asked.
"Of course, vicar," replied the woman, "just a little wind."
The next time the vicar saw the two women, they were walking down the High Street, pushing a pram. He stopped to say hello and bending down to look in the pram, remarked
"So that's the little fart, is it?"

★ ★ ★

A wife is so distressed at her husband's excessive drinking that she decides to try and scare him into stopping. After pub closing time that night, she waits for him in the church graveyard, crouched down behind one of the tombstones. Sure enough, he takes the short cut home and as he staggers past her, she jumps up in full devil's costume and shouts
"Beware, beware, Arthur Chivers, carry on drinking as you are, and you'll soon be joining me down below!"
"What!" he exclaimed, somewhat befuddled, "who are you?"
"I am the devil himself," she boomed.
The drunk began to smile and held out his hand to greet him.
"Well I never," he says, "you'll know me then, I'm married to your sister."

★ ★ ★

The bishop was not looking forward to his meeting with the new vicar. The latter had only been in his parish a few weeks, but already there were many complaints.

"So why did you decide to enter the ministry?" asked the bishop.

"I was called," replied the vicar.

"Mmm," mused the bishop. "Are you absolutely sure? Maybe you were mistaken and it was another sound you heard."

★ ★ ★

A couple were enjoying the concert when two nuns came and sat down in front of them, their hats totally obscuring the couple's view.

"If we were watching this in Holland where there aren't many nuns, we probably wouldn't get any in front of us," complained the man loudly.

"China would be even better," replied the woman.

They continued muttering for five minutes until one of the nuns turned round and said calmly,

"Why don't you both go to hell, you won't find any nuns down there."

★ ★ ★

The vicar is preparing for the morning service when he spots a woman, in a very short skirt, sitting in the front pew. He beckons to his deacon and asks

"Isn't that Fanny Blue?"

"Oh no, I don't think so," replies the deacon. "It's just the way the light is reflected through the stained glass window."

★ ★ ★

A nun met a man walking along with a number of game birds slung over his shoulder.

"I'm afraid all the pheasants are taken," he told the nun, "but you can have this bugarin bird, here."

"Oh!" exclaimed the nun, horrified, "please don't curse in that way."

"No, no," replied the man quickly, "that's what this bird is called. It's a bugarin bird and it's very tasty."

So the nun took the bird back to the convent and showed it to the Mother Superior.

"Look what I have," she said. "It's a bugarin bird and it'll make a good meal when the priest comes round tonight."

"Sister, how could you!" exclaimed the Mother Superior, "how dare you use such filthy language!"

"Oh no, I didn't swear," assured the nun. "That's its name, a bugarin bird."

So the bird was taken to the kitchen for cooking.

That evening, the nuns sat down to dinner with the priest as their guest.

"What a delicious bird," he commented.

"Thank you," they replied.

"I was given the bugarin bird by one of the local hunters," said the nun.

"And I thought the bugarin bird would be a welcome change to this evening's meal," said the Mother Superior.

"And I cooked the bugarin bird," added another nun.

The priest was greatly shocked by their conversation and replied angrily, "Well let's eat the fucking thing, shall we?"

★ ★ ★

"Okay girls," said the priest at confession, "one at a time please." The first girl went in and confessed she'd kissed a man the night before. She was told to wash her lips in Holy Water.

The second girl went in and confessed she'd touched a man's penis. As she left the confessional, she told the others she had to wash her hands in Holy Water.

Suddenly an almighty row broke out between the remaining two girls and the priest came running from his box.

"My goodness!" he exclaimed, "girls, girls, what's going on?"

One of the girls retorted hotly, "if I'm going to have to gargle the Holy Water, I'm sure as hell going to do it before she has to put her arse in it."

★ ★ ★

The curvaceous woman arrived at the church door topless.

"I'm afraid you can't come in here," exclaimed the vicar.

"But I've got a divine right!" she protested.

"I agree," he said, "and a divine left as well, but I can't let you in."

★ ★ ★

The priest and the C of E vicar bumped into each other in the public library.

"What a coincidence," said the vicar. "I had a dream last night about a Catholic heaven. It was full of people, drinking, singing and dancing."

"Really," replied the priest. "I had a dream about a protestant heaven. It was very peaceful, beautiful countryside, gorgeous gardens and gently flowing streams."

The vicar smiled contentedly. "And what were the people doing?"

"What people?" replied the priest.

★ ★ ★

A vain middle aged woman went to confession.

"Forgive me Father for I have sinned. I spent an hour this morning in front of the mirror admiring my beautiful body. Will I have to do a penance?"

"No, no," said the priest. "You only do a penance when you have done something wrong. Not for a mistake."

★ ★ ★

For as long as he could remember, the priest had tried to get his next door neighbour to come to church.

"It's no good, Father," he would say. "I just don't believe and nothing you can say will change my mind."

It just so happened that one day the priest and his next door neighbour found themselves aboard the same flight to Rome. Unfortunately, an hour out of Heathrow, the plane developed engine trouble and the situation looked very dangerous. The priest immediately crossed himself and began praying. But then he was astonished to see his neighbour cross himself as well. Happily, the situation was not as grave as anticipated and the plane made a safe landing. As they left the airport, the priest turned to his neighbour and said

"Even though you've always told me you don't believe, when the chips are down, you turn to God."

"Oh no, not at all," replied the neighbour. "I'm a door-to-door salesman and before I face any unknown situation I always check I'm prepared – glasses, flies, money and pen."

★ ★ ★

The new vicar set out on his parish rounds to introduce himself to the congregation. At his second stop he came across a cottage standing alone, with six children of all ages, running around madly in the garden. He knocked at the door, but getting no answer, peered through the dining room window.

"Oh goodness!" he exclaimed, moving away hurriedly from the sight of two naked bodies writhing around in ecstasy. Blushing profusely, he moved on to the next cottage where he met a friendly man hanging out the washing. After a few moments of chat, he commented on the people next door.

"They really love children, don't they?" remarked the vicar.

"You can say that again," replied the man, "his wife's just gone into hospital to have her seventh, so my wife's gone round to see if there's anything she can do to help."

★ ★ ★

The Mother Superior lay very ill in bed. Three doctors had visited but failed to make her better. Eventually, they called in a Chinese medicine man who told her she was suffering from a lack of sexual activity and unless she released these pent up frustrations, she would die.

"Oh, but I can't," she gasped. "It's against everything I stand for."

But again, the medicine man warned her of the consequences and eventually she gave in.

"I must insist on three conditions," she said. "First, he must be blind so that he will never recognise me. Secondly, he must be dumb so that he can never speak about it."

"As you wish," said the Chinese medicine man. "But what is the third condition?"

There was a long pause and then she said

"He must have a big dick."

★　★　★

A nun walked into an off license and asked the owner for a bottle of five star brandy.

"Well, I'm not sure," began the owner, "it's a bit unusual to sell a sister of the church some alcohol."

"Oh don't worry," she assured him. "The bottle's for medical purposes. It's our Mother Superior, she's suffering badly from constipation."

"Well in that case, I'm happy to," said the owner, wrapping up his finest bottle of brandy. A couple of hours later, he closed the shop and set off for home when he saw a figure

slouched up against the wall. As he got nearer, he realised it was the nun, half-sozzled with a three-quarter-empty brandy bottle at her feet. "Hey!" he cried angrily, "look at the state of you. I only gave you the brandy because you told me it was for your Mother Superior's constipation."

"That's right," she slurred, "it is. When she sees the state of me, she'll shit herself."

★ ★ ★

"Excuse me vicar," said the man as he walked into church. "I've had my bicycle stolen and I wonder if you would mention in your sermon today how wrong it is to steal."

"Why certainly," replied the vicar. "As it happens, I shall be talking about the ten commandments so that will fit in nicely.

"And so I say to you, remember what God taught us. Thou shalt not kill, thou shalt not steal..." Later that week the vicar bumped into the man again as he was wheeling his bicycle down the road.

"Ah, I see my sermon must have worked," remarked the vicar.

"Oh no, it wasn't that," replied the man. It was when you mentioned, "Thou shalt not commit adultery that I remembered where I'd left it."

★ ★ ★

MEET THE CON ARTIST

The salesman of the year was determined to sell the cheap suit to the hesitant customer.

"But the left trouser leg is shorter than the right," he remarked.

"But that's why it's so cheap sir. All you need do is bend the right knee a bit and no one will notice the difference."

"But look at the two sides of the jacket, one's two inches longer than the other."

"Not to worry, sir, just pull this side up a bit and tuck it under your chin. Now they're equal. And remember, the suit's very cheap, so lift up your left shoulder and then the sleeve won't hang over your hand."

Eventually the customer was satisfied and he bought the suit, choosing to wear it home. As he left the shop, he passed two doctors coming in and when they saw the man limping along with his shoulder in the air and his chin tucked down on his chest, one remarked to the other

"Poor man, he's got a terrible affliction."

"Indeed," agreed the other, "but they've managed to fit the suit perfectly."

★ ★ ★

Just as the man was going into the bar, a crocodile tapped him on the shoulder.

"Fancy making some quick money?" he hissed.

"Bloody hell, a talking crocodile!" he exclaimed. "I can't believe it."

"Sshh," whispered the crocodile, "now listen to me. We'll go into the bar and you bet everyone in there that I can talk. It can't fail." The man was delighted with the idea, so he carried out the plan, took everyone's money and then asked the crocodile to speak. Silence. It didn't say a word. Eventually the man had to pay out hundreds of pounds before storming out of the pub, seething with rage.

"You fucking wanker," he yelled at the crocodile, "you've cost me a fortune and I'm going to make a handbag out of you, RIGHT NOW!".

"Calm down, calm down," replied the crocodile. "When we go back in there tomorrow, just imagine the odds we'll get."

★ ★ ★

The East End gang boss had always been very careful whom he employed, for fear of being grassed up. He thought he'd been really clever with his crooked accountant who was deaf and dumb. There wasn't much of a risk that he would overhear too much. However, it eventually dawned on the boss that someone was stealing money from him. A lot of money! And it didn't take long for him to discover it was his crooked accountant.

"Benny," he ordered, "Get that bastard down here pronto and

get Marty to come with him. He can read the hand signs."

Later in his office, the boss stated interrogating him.

"Marty, ask him what he's done with the money."

At first the terrified accountant signalled his ignorance of the theft but when a gun was put to his head, he spilled the beans. With rapid hand movements, he explained that he'd hidden all the money in a trunk in an old derelict factory, two miles from the office.

"So what did he say?" demanded the boss impatiently.

Marty thought quickly and replied

"It's no good boss. He says you haven't got the bottle to shoot him."

★ ★ ★

"Hey! That bottle of magic potion you sold me was supposed to make me more intelligent... I'm beginning to think it's a big con."

"There, you see! You're more intelligent already."

★ ★ ★

The Lord of the Bowertree estate was entertaining an important guest for lunch. He asked his manservant to pop down to the station to collect a parcel containing a special bottle of the finest malt whisky and a box of Havana cigars.

"By the way," he told his manservant, "I've run out of snuff. Pop into the tobacconist's, there's a good chap."

An hour later the manservant was returning from the village when he realised he'd forgotten the snuff.

"Bugger," he muttered to himself, looking around for inspiration. Suddenly, he spotted an old cow pat in the grass, it had dried up in the warm sun and turned white and crumbly. Quick as a flash, he picked it up, crumpled it into fine dust and decided to take a chance.

After lunch, the Lord called for his manservant.

"Ah, there you are," he beamed, "a little whisky, a fine cigar and a pinch of snuff."

As the manservant did as he was asked, the Lord sniffed the air suspiciously.

"There's an odd smell in here," he said, "has anyone brought something in on their shoes?"

"No," came the reply from his eminent guest, "actually I've got a bit of a cold, so I can't smell anything."

"Then take some snuff," said the Lord handing him the casket.

After a good couple of sniffs, the guest sat back and remarked, "That must be good snuff, Cecil. It's cleared my nose wonderfully, and I can smell that shit now."

★ ★ ★

A man walked up to the bar and the landlord said

"Good evening sir, would you like a drink?"

"A whisky, please."

The landlord poured the drink, handed it to the man and said

"That'll be £1.50, please."

"Oh no," replied the man. "You invited me to have a drink. I'm not paying."

There followed a lively argument when a man sitting close by interrupted them.

"Excuse me, I have legal experience and this customer is well within his rights not to pay."

"Right," roared the landlord. "Drink up and get out, you're banned."

The customer left, but ten minutes later returned.

"I told you to get out and never come back," said the landlord angrily.

"But I've never been in here before," protested the customer.

The landlord faltered. "Oh... sorry... you must have a double."

"Well thank you very much," replied the customer, "and one here for my legal friend."

★ ★ ★

A real sleaze is touring the nightclubs, looking for a bit of skirt. In his pocket is a frog. Eventually he finds a girl on her own and gets chatting. They have a few drinks together and when she is totally relaxed, he gets out his frog.

"Here," he whispers, "I've got something special to show you. This frog eats pussy."

The girl is shocked at this piece of news but after a few more drinks, her curiosity is aroused so she goes back to his flat. She lies on the bed, legs apart, and the man puts the frog between them. However nothing happens. The frog just sits there.

"Okay, okay, my little friend," says the man, dropping his trousers, I'll show you just one more time."

★ ★ ★

A variety show producer is on the look-out for a new act, and one day he happens to be walking round a country fair when he notices a group of people huddled around one particular stall. As he approaches, he sees a chicken dancing up and down on an old ceramic pot. The audience are obviously enjoying the act, so the producer asks the man if the chicken is for sale. After a lot of hard bargaining, they eventually decide on a sum of £1,500 and the producer goes off happily, with the chicken and the pot safely under his arm. However, two days later he storms back in a very angry mood.

"You double-crossing bastard," yells the producer. "You tricked me, that chicken hasn't danced a step since I bought him."

"Mmm," mused the man, thoughtfully. "I bet you didn't light the candle under the pot."

★ ★ ★

A man was desperate to buy a singing canary, but none of the shops for miles around had one in stock. Eventually, he was advised to buy a mavi bird.

"If you file the bird's beak down by 3/8", it'll sing just like a canary," he was told. "But be very careful, any more than that, and the bird will die because he won't be able to eat."

So the man went to the hardware shop and bought a file and a steel tape measure. A few weeks later, he happened to go back to the shop for some nails and the storekeeper gave him a friendly greeting.

"Hello sir, I remember you. You had a mavi bird, how is it?" The man looked downcast and answered, "the poor thing's dead."

"Oh, I am sorry. Did you file too much off the beak?"

"Oh no. He was dead when I got him out of the vice."

★ ★ ★

A man went to a brothel and asked how much they charged.

"£30 when you start and £40 when you finish," he was told. That sounded all right to him, so he went in and did the business.

The following week he returned for a repeat performance.

"£30 when I start and £40 when I finish. Is that right?" he asked and on confirmation he handed over £30 and was taken upstairs to see Lil. Nearly two hours later he was still on the job and Lil began to complain loudly.

"Now listen," she said. "You're taking the mickey here. Ain't it about time, you scarpered."

"Oh no, dear lady," he replied, "I can't. You see, I'm broke."

★ ★ ★

Two skinflints decided to put a small wager on their game of golf. £1 to the winner was agreed and they set off. By the end of the sixth tee, all was equal, but then Clive hooked his ball into the rough. Try as they could, there was no sign of his ball, and it would mean that Clive would drop at least two strokes. Thinking of the wager they'd put on the game, he waited for Gerald to turn his back, then took out a second ball, dropped it on the grass and shouted in triumph.

"Ah, found it at last, here it is."

"Why Clive, you're a bloody cheat," said Malcolm angrily. "That's not your ball, there's no length you won't go to just to win the bet."

"Now look here," blustered Clive. "How do you know, it's not my ball."

"Because I've been standing on it for the past five minutes," replied Malcolm.

★ ★ ★

"I'm sorry Dave," said Lucy, "but it's over. I've tried to make it work but I just can't make myself love you."

"Oh no," cried Dave, putting his head in his hands, "Lucy, I'm devastated. I had such great plans for us, particularly now I've inherited a country mansion from my spinster aunt."

"Well, I guess I could try again," she replied quickly.

★ ★ ★

MEET THE COUPLE

The man went for his annual check up and was given a clean bill of health by the doctor.

"There is just one thing," he said. "You are a bit smelly down below, if you know what I mean."

Exceedingly embarrassed, the man went home and as he walked through the door, he shouted to his wife.

"Hold on," she called out from upstairs. "I'm so busy, I haven't even got time to wipe my bum."

"That's what I want to talk to you about," he said.

★ ★ ★

The man turned to his wife in anger and said
"You silly cow, locking the dog in the boot of the car has got to be the most stupid thing ever."
"Oh yeah," she retorted, "wait till I tell you about the car keys."

★ ★ ★

The couple had been married for seven years and were going through a bad patch. They agreed to see a marriage counsellor and a few minutes into the interview, the counsellor took the wife in his arms and kissed her passionately.

"Now, that's what your wife needs," he explained to the astonished husband. "More passion. Tuesday, Thursday and Friday every week."

The husband thought for a moment and replied grudgingly

"Well, okay then. But I can't bring her in on Fridays, it's darts night."

★ ★ ★

A married couple are driving down the interstate doing 55 mph. The wife is behind the wheel. Her husband looks over at her and says

"Honey, I know we've been married for 15 years, but, I want a divorce."

The wife says nothing but slowly increases speed to 60 mph. He then says

"I don't want you to try to talk me out of it, because I've been having an affair with your best friend, and she's a better lover than you."

Again the wife stays quiet and just speeds up as her anger increases.

"I want the house," he says.

Again the wife speeds up, and is now doing 70mph.

"I want the kids too," he says.

The wife just keeps driving faster and faster – now she's up to 80mph.

"I want the car, the checking account, and all the credit cards too," he continues.

The wife slowly starts to veer toward a bridge overpass piling, as he says

"Is there anything you want?"
"No, I've got everything I need," says the wife.
"What's that?" he asks.
The wife replies, just before they hit the wall at 90mph,
"I've got the airbag!"

★ ★ ★

The husband was coming up to retirement age, and his wife decided they should celebrate by taking a week's cruise to the continent.

"We can pretend we're young again," she said coyly, "and do all the things that we used to do when we first met."

The husband agreed and while his wife made the arrangements, he visited the local chemist for a box of condoms and a packet of seasick tablets. However, when he returned, his wife greeted him with the news that if they booked up for one week, they'd get another week free. So back to the chemist he went, to get another packet of condoms and more seasick pills. Saturday night arrived and to the couple's joy, they won £1 million on the lottery.

"Oh Charles," beamed his wife, "now we can do what we've always wanted to do, and take our dream round-the-world cruise."

"Yes dear," replied Charles as he put on his hat and headed for the door.

"Won't be long," he shouted.

"Twelve packets of condoms and six bottles of seasick pills, please," he asked the chemist.

"You know sir," said the chemist, "I don't mean to pry, but if it makes you that sick, why do you keep on doing it?"

★ ★ ★

Randy Ron, his workmates called him. He just couldn't get enough.

One afternoon he came home early from work, went straight up to the bedroom to change and found his wife in bed with the covers pulled right over her head. Not one to miss a chance, he stripped off, crept under the covers and hastily made love to her. Later he got up and went downstairs, only to discover his wife in the garden.

"How can this be," he demanded, "I just left you in bed."

"No, that's my mother, she wasn't feeling so well so I told her to lie down."

The man turned pale and sat down shaking.

"Bloody hell, I've just made love to your mother!"

"Oh no," she gasped, running upstairs. "Mum, Mum, why didn't you say something?"

Her mother replied with affront, "I haven't spoken to that randy bugger for three years and I'm not about to start now."

★ ★ ★

A married couple decided to join a nudist colony and after their initial embarrassment, they settled down quite happily. At dinner that night, she said to her husband, "I'm glad we chose to do this. It feels right, it gives me a nice warm feeling."

"I'm not surprised," he replied. "You've got your tits in the soup."

★ ★ ★

The old couple had been married for more than 40 years and their sex life was sadly lacking. Hoping that a change of scenery might do the trick, they took a holiday to North Africa and while Bob dozed in bed, Mabel went shopping in the local markets. On one occasion she was fascinated to watch a snake charmer. As he played the flute, the snake would emerge from the basket until it was standing straight in the air. I must have that, she thought, so after a great deal of haggling she finally bought the flute and hurried back to the hotel. Bob was fast asleep when Mabel returned, so she quietly got out the flute and started to play it. Slowly, slowly, the bedclothes started to rise until they were nearly a foot above her sleeping husband. Overcome with anticipation, Mabel tore her clothes off and threw back the bedclothes, to find her husband's pajama cord standing to attention.

★ ★ ★

An old country couple visit the doctor in the nearby town. Neither of them had been inside a surgery for more than 20 years, so it was all a bit strange.

"Right, Mrs Crotchitt, before I do the examination, I'll need a specimen. If you'll just return to the waiting room, it won't be long," said the doctor.

Baffled, she returns to her husband and tells him about the specimen. "What can it be?" she asks puzzled.

"I don't know," he replies. "Why don't you see if you can find that nice nurse who showed us in here. I'm sure she'll tell you."

So the old lady goes off and after a few minutes, an almighty noise breaks out. There are sounds of broken glass and raised voices. Suddenly the old woman returns looking very dishevelled.

"Bloody hell, woman, what happened to you," asks her husband.

"I don't rightly know," replies the distraught wife. "I went and asked the nurse what a specimen was. She told me to piss in a bottle, I told her to crap in a bucket and then things just got out of hand."

★ ★ ★

The marriage of the two celebrities had become public property, so it wasn't a surprise that the intimate details of their divorce were splashed across the tabloid press. The most juicy piece of news for the readers was that they'd split up because his todger was too small to satisfy the needs of his beautiful wife. The rowing couple met for the last time in court, their hostility to each other was plainly obvious.

As she got up to leave she turned to him and putting her little finger in the air, hissed, "Good riddance, creep."

He responded immediately. He put a finger in both sides of his mouth and stretched it as wide as possible. "So long, bitch," he snarled.

★ ★ ★

The young fireman was being severely tested by his new wife. Night and morning she would demand sex but whatever he did, or however hard he tried, she was never satisfied.

"More rope, more rope," she would urge. He would try his best but again she would call out "more rope, more rope."

The poor man was so disheartened he thrust his balls up as well.

"Better, better," she called out, "but not so many knots please."

★ ★ ★

The middle-aged couple stopped overnight in an hotel and just after midnight, as they were lying in bed, they heard terrific noises from the room next door. A girl seemed to be pounding the bed and moaning loudly.

"Ooh Marvin, it sounds as if she's having a fit," said Agnes.

"Oh yes," replied Marvin, thinking back to their early days of marriage, "and it sounds like a bloody tight one too."

★ ★ ★

Martin arrived back from the doctors feeling very miserable. The doctor had told him that unless he lost two stone in weight, he was in danger of having a heart attack.

Now his wife loved him very much and realised that it was going to be very hard for him to cut down on his eating. So she decided to shame him into it.

"I bet you won't do it," she sneered, "you're too weak willed. Look at Geoffrey, he's given up smoking, but then he's much more determined."

Martin was angry. "Right," he blustered, "if that's what you think of me, I'll show you. Not only will I lose two stone but until I do, sex is out."

To her dismay, Martin moved into the spare room that night and two weeks later he was still there. His wife was so miserable. She missed her husband terribly, so on the following night, after he'd gone to bed, she knocked on the door.

"It's only me, can I come in a moment," she said.

Martin couldn't believe his eyes when she walked through the door. There she stood in a silky dressing gown which fell open as she moved to reveal her nakedness underneath. She looked at him coyly from beneath her long eyelashes and whispered huskily "Hello Martin."

"What do you want?" he replied, gasping for breath.

"I just wanted to let you know that Geoffrey's started smoking again."

* * *

"Carol, Carol," whispered her husband urgently. "This bloody house is haunted."

"Go back to sleep," said his wife.

"You're dreaming."

"No, I'm serious, it's true. I just went to the bathroom and when I got there, the light went on by itself, and when I came out, it turned itself off."

"Oh no," groaned his wife. "You bloody prat. You've pissed in the refrigerator again."

* * *

A couple who had been married for nearly twenty years decided to go on a cycling holiday, hoping it would help repair a very shaky marriage. On the second day, they found themselves high up on the moors in heavy rain, when the husband's back tyre had a puncture. Try as he may, he could not find the damaged part of the tyre and the wife remarked scornfully

"I knew it, you're bloody hopeless. If the hole had been surrounded by hair, you'd have found it fast enough."

★ ★ ★

The woman picked the phone up and a voice said
"Hello Sandy, fancy a drink tonight?"
"No, I'm working late," she replied.
"Well, how about tomorrow?"
"No, I'm meeting friends for dinner."
"Okay, let's make it this weekend?"
"Sorry, I'm off to my mother's."
"Oh for goodness sake. Sometimes I wonder why we ever got married!"

★ ★ ★

Watching her husband dish up second helpings onto his plate, she said scornfully

"Sometimes, I think you like food more than you like sex."

"Now why would you think that," he replied, munching away happily, "We're the only couple I know, who have mirrors on the dining room ceiling!"

★ ★ ★

A middle-aged couple went on their second honeymoon to Texas. They spent a great first week but then disaster struck. A pickpocket stole the man's wallet and with it all their holiday money. Fearing they would have to cut their holiday short, they were just packing their suitcases when the husband noticed a poster on the wall. It was advertising a local rodeo. First prize for the person who could stay on the bucking bronco longest, was the equivalent of £10,000.

"That's it!" he cried. Before the wife could question him, he hurried down to the rodeo and signed up. To everyone's amazement, this complete stranger beat every other contestant and walked away with the prize. The man's wife was amazed.

"But Jack, you've never been on a horse in your life. How did you manage it?"

"Don't you remember when we went on our honeymoon, Doris, and you had that awful cough?" he replied.

★ ★ ★

"You're so bloody frigid, I wouldn't be surprised if you put cold cream between your legs," he shouted angrily to his wife.

"Oh very funny," retorted his wife, "and I wouldn't be surprised if you put vanishing cream between yours."

★ ★ ★

One night, as a couple was going to bed, a burglar forced his way into the house and tied them up.

"Listen," hissed her pathetic husband, "do whatever he says or he might hurt us. If he wants you to have sex, then just agree." "Okay darling," she replied, "but I did overhear him say he thought you were cute."

★ ★ ★

There was a man who was married to such a beautiful girl that he was the envy of his mates in the pub. One lunch-time one of the blokes said to him

"Listen Ted, I'll give you £200 if I could just feel your wife's tits."

The band was outraged, but when he told his wife she asked him to reconsider.

"Think about it darling," she said. "What's a quick feel of my tits when we could put that £200 down as a deposit on a holiday."

The husband eventually relented and the bloke came round the next day. She stripped off her blouse and bra and stood there waiting for him to fondle them.

"Aah," he sighed in satisfaction. "What a beautiful sight. They're so perfect, so smooth, so round..."

"Come on man," said the husband impatiently, "get on and feel them."

"Oh no," he replied. "I don't need to feel them now, besides it would cost me £200."

★ ★ ★

MEET THE DENTIST

The dentist looked at his patient and gave his verdict.

"For the very best results, your treatment will cost about £5,000, but," he added hastily, "you will have perfect teeth for the rest of your life."

"Oh dear!" exclaimed the patient, "that's an awful lot of money. I couldn't pay it all in one go."

"No, no, I quite understand, we could arrange monthly payments."

"I see. I suppose it would be a bit like buying a luxury item, like a yacht," mused the man.

"Yes, I am," replied the dentist.

★ ★ ★

"Come in Donald," said the dentist, "take a seat. Now, I wonder if you'll do something for me. Before we start, would you mind yelling very loudly?"

Donald looked puzzled. "Well, I suppose so," he replied, "but can you tell me why?"

"By all means," replied the dentist. "My team's got through to the FA Cup Final, but if I don't get rid of that full waiting room out there, I'll never get to see them."

★ ★ ★

"I wish you hadn't left it for so long before coming to see me," said the dentist to his patient. "But your teeth are way past being saved, so I'll have to take them all out and make you a set of false ones." The patient looked terrified.

"I can't," he gasped. "I just can't stand the pain."

"Come now," said the dentist impatiently. "Just imagine how nice it will be again to be able to eat your food properly. And I can assure you there'll be very little pain."

The man still didn't look convinced.

"I tell you what," said the dentist, who'd just had an idea, "why don't you talk to Mr Taylor. He lives down your street and I did the same for him not so long ago. If you ask him about the pain, I'm positive he'll reassure you."

So later in the week, the man contacted Mr Taylor and asked him about the pain.

"Mmm," mused Mr Taylor, "let me put it this way. I had my teeth done four months ago and last week I was repairing our garden gate when I accidentally hammered a nail into my hand. And that was the first time in four months my teeth didn't hurt!"

★ ★ ★

"Kate, listen to me," pleaded her dentist. "We've got to stop this. It'll only end in tears."

"But why?" she asked. "We've had great sex for over a year and my husband's never found out. He's not even suspicious."

"But he will be soon. Don't you realise you've only got one tooth left in your mouth."

★ ★ ★

Instead of opening his mouth, Colin pulled down his trousers to expose his todger.

"Now hold on a minute," said the dentist looking alarmed. "I'm not a doctor, I can't help you down there."

"Oh yes you can," replied the man, "take a closer look. I've got a tooth stuck in it."

★ ★ ★

"Thanks for seeing us so quickly," said the grateful man to the dentist. "As I said on the phone, it's a bit of an emergency because this toothache's come just as we were flying out to the Bahamas at 6 o'clock tonight. Please take it out as quickly as possible. Don't worry about pain killers or anything like that, just yank it out."

"Well, I think I ought to warn you that it will be very painful if I don't use anything."

"Not to worry. Just get a move on."

"Okay. I think you're very brave. Just pop up into the chair for me please."

The man turned to his wife and said

"You heard what he said, Ruth, sit up in the chair."

★ ★ ★

"I'm not paying this outrageous bill," yelled the man. "You've charged me four times over."

"Maybe so," replied the dentist calmly, "but you made so much noise during your treatment, that the other three patients in the waiting room, cancelled their appointments and have gone elsewhere."

★ ★ ★

MEET THE FARMER

The farm inspector was on his annual tour of the county and had arrived at Farmer Giles' place.

"So how many sheep do you have?" he asked.

"I don't know," replied the farmer, "every time I try to count them, I fall asleep."

★ ★ ★

A motorist was driving through farm country when he got a terrible urge to have a shit. He spotted a man up ahead ploughing the field, so he told him his predicament and the farmer pointed to some outbuildings 200 yards away.

"You'll find a privy up there," he said, "but watch out for..." But the man was off and running so he didn't hear the end of the sentence. Sprinting up the field behind him the farmer turned the corner, only to see the poor man had fallen into a trench.

"That's what I was trying to warn you about," he said.

"Oh, it doesn't matter," replied the man. "I wouldn't have made it anyway."

★ ★ ★

"That bloody bull's going to the knacker's yard," yelled the farmer. "It's nearly killed me three times."
"Oh give him one more chance," replied his wife.

★ ★ ★

The young man had been brought up in the city. He'd never seen the countryside, he'd never come across any of the animals. It so happened that one weekend he was invited to go camping with some friends. He set off early in his car and arranged to meet them at the farmer's field. Alas, just half a mile from his destination, a goat ran out into the road and he ran over it, killing it stone dead. Overcome with shock, he finished his journey and sought out the old farmer.

"I've just run over something, back there down the lane," he said pointing. "But I'm not sure what it was."

The farmer asked him to describe it.

"Well, it had a beard, two tits and smelt dreadful."

"Oh no," wailed the farmer, "you've just killed my wife."

★ ★ ★

A kindly man came across a young boy whose cart had shed its load of manure.

"Come back with me," he said, "we'll get you cleaned up, have a spot of lunch then I'll bring back my two sons to help you clear the road."

The boy hesitated, "I'm not sure," he faltered, "my dad might not like that."

"I think your dad will be pleased you're doing something about it," said the man and eventually the boy was persuaded. A couple of hours later, they returned with his two sons to begin clearing the load.

"By the way, where is your dad?" asked the man.

"Under the manure," came the reply.

★ ★ ★

Two chickens were standing at the side of the road. One said to the other

"For goodness sake, don't cross that road otherwise everyone will want to know why."

★ ★ ★

A farmer was bemoaning the fact that his rooster had died and he was having trouble with his chickens.

"Listen Fred, you can have mine," said a neighbouring farmer. "He's bloody sex mad, in fact he's worn my chickens out so I'm happy to sell him."

So the rooster is bought and taken back to the farm where he immediately disappears into the hen house and isn't seen again for three days. Within a few weeks, the hens are thriving, as are the ducks, geese and any other passing animal. Then, to the farmer's distress, the rooster goes missing and after searching for him for a couple of hours, he eventually finds him in the far field, lying on his back with his feet in the air.

**"Oh no!" gasps the farmer, "the poor bugger's overdone it."
"Shshsh," hisses the rooster. "I'm just playing dead, see that
big vulture up there?"**

★ ★ ★

A cattle feed merchant was visiting Lower Brook Farm when
a pig hobbled by with a wooden leg. He turned to the farmer
and enquired

"Why has that pig got a wooden leg?"

"Oh, you mean old Maurice. What a pig!" enthused the farmer.
"He's a real hero. Last month, he saved my youngest from certain
death. He was playing in the long grass and if the pig hadn't
squeaked just as I was backing my tractor into the field, I'd have
surely gone over him."

"Yes, yes," said the merchant impatiently.

"But why has it got a wooden leg?"

By this time, the farmer was in full flow. "... and then last week,
it saw off a fox before it could get to my chickens."

"Yes, very good," said the merchant.

"But why has it got a wooden leg?"

"Well, for goodness sake!" he exclaimed. "After all that pig has
done, we couldn't eat him in one go."

★ ★ ★

**A ventriloquist, taking his young family on a trip round a
local farm, decided to have some fun.**

"This ere's the pigs," said the farm worker.

"Hello," said the pigs (in fact it was the ventriloquist throwing his voice.)

The farm worker looked astounded and hastily moved on.

"Them's the horses," he said, pointing to two animals peering over the fence.

"Hello children," said the horses, "tell him to give us some better hay, this lot's awful."

This time the farm worker looked very worried.

"Now look 'ere," he said desperately, "when we visit the goats, don't you believe anything they tell you."

★ ★ ★

The council officer had to make his annual visit to some of the remote farms in his area. By lunch-time, he had arrived at Grimes Bottom and as he walked up the private road, he saw the farmer in the outlying field, shagging a goat. Hastily moving on, he spotted the son shagging a sheep. Then as he rounded the corner he caught sight of the old grandfather, tossing himself off behind the barn. Seething with anger, he stormed up to the farmhouse door and knocked loudly. When the wife opened up, he vented his anger on her.

"I've just walked up the lane and I've seen your husband shagging a goat, your son shagging a sheep and your father tossing himself off. Words fail me! What do you have to say about it?"

"I understand how you feel," she said sadly, "but old age has caught up with my father and he's too old to go chasing animals anymore."

★ ★ ★

A group of ramblers were walking through the countryside when they came across a farmer ploughing his field. Strangely enough, the farmer was naked from the waist down.

"Excuse me Farmer," they said, "may we ask why you're only half dressed."

"Well it's like this," he answered. "Last week was very hot and on Tuesday I spent most of the day up in the top field without my shirt on. Bugger me! Did I suffer the next day. My neck was as stiff as a plank. So this is my wife's idea."

★ ★ ★

Three bulls had serviced the farmer's herd of cows for more than five years. During that time they had split the herd between them, each having an amount appropriate to their size, so the biggest bull had 20 more than the smallest.

Then one day, the bulls discovered a fourth bull was going to join them.

"Sod that," said the biggest bull, "he's not having any of my cows," and the others agreed they were not sharing either. The following morning a huge lorry arrived at the gate of the field and out stormed the largest bull ever seen. He snorted loudly and looked around arrogantly.

"Oh well," said the biggest bull nervously, "I guess he can have a few of my cows. It'll be nice not to have to work so hard."

"Yeah, I agree," said the middle-sized bull, "there's no reason why we can't share a bit. He can have some of mine.

Suddenly the smallest bull started snorting and stamping his feet on the earth, sending up clouds of dust.

"Hey, listen mate," hissed the other two, "I wouldn't go up against him, just let him have some of your cows."

"He can have all my fucking cows," replied the bull. "I just want him to know I'm a bull!"

★ ★ ★

A travelling salesman was returning home very late one night when his car broke down on the middle of Dartmoor. He needed to use a phone and as he peered across the huge desolate landscape he spotted the silhouette of a farmhouse nestling in a valley.

The salesman headed off towards the house but as he got closer, he suddenly had doubts.

"Oh bugger," he thought. "The farmer's not going to be too pleased to see me at this time of night, he's probably asleep."

He continued on and had ever darker thoughts, "...might even think I'm a burglar and turn his gun on me."

By this time, he'd reached the door and rung the bell. After a short time, he heard footsteps coming down the stairs and he thought again. "Shit, he might just set the dogs on me."

In the silence of the night came the sound of the key turning in the lock, and as the door started to open, the traveller said loudly "Oh fuck your bloody phone."

★ ★ ★

A farmer was preparing to mow the paddock when he heard a voice saying "Please don't cut my buttercups, I implore you."

Looking round he saw a beautiful maiden in a long flowing dress with a garland of buttercups in her golden hair.

"I am the guardian of the countryside," she told him, "and if you leave them to grow, I will guarantee you an endless supply of butter for the rest of your life."

The farmer looked at her and replied peevishly, "why couldn't you have been here last week when I was cutting down the pussy willow."

★ ★ ★

The President was driving through Republican country when his driver knocked over and killed a pig that suddenly strayed into the middle of the road.

"You'd better go and tell the farmer," ordered the President, "and offer to pay for it."

"Yes sir," replied the driver and off he went.

It was almost four hours later when he returned with a satisfied look on his face.

"Where the hell have you been?" demanded the President angrily.

"Well, I did as you said. I went up to the farmer's house and told him what I'd done. He invited me in, gave me a fantastic meal and then invited me upstairs to shag his daughter."

"But why?" puzzled the President.

"I've no idea," replied the driver. "All I said was that I was the President's driver and I'd run over the pig."

★ ★ ★

Two farmers are taking their sheep to market when the brake fails on their truck and they are unable to take the next bend safely. Instead they crash through a fence and end up teetering on the edge of a precipice.

"Quick Jeff," says one, "let's get out of here."

"What about the sheep?" asks Jeff.

"Oh fuck the sheep," he replies.

"Really! Do you think we have time?"

★ ★ ★

MEET THE GOOD TIME GIRLS

The regiment headed back for the nearest town after two weeks of manoeuvres in the mountains. As they arrived, the commanding officer asked his sergeant Ron Cox, to do a recce of the town to find out if there was any spare overnight accommodation.

"Meanwhile, I'll take the troops up to that big house on the hill," said the Commanding Officer, "and see if I can find anything up there." The forty men dismounted at the door of the big house which was, in fact, the local brothel. The C.O. rang the bell and a moment later, it was answered by the Madam.

"Yes, can I help you?"

The C.O. explained the situation.

"So how many are you?" she enquired.

"Forty, without Cox," he replied.

"Oh no," she laughed, "you've got to be joking."

★   ★   ★

A man has only got an hour left before he has to rejoin his ship, so he hurries off to the local brothel for a 'quickie'.

"You'll have to wait," replies the Madam, "we've got the girls, but there isn't a room free."

"Forget the room we'll find somewhere. Just get me the girl," he replies.

So he and Susie climb up the fire escape and find a space on the flat roof. However they get so carried away that they roll too close to the edge and both of them plunge to the ground entwined, where they are killed stone dead.

Moments later, an old drunk tramp staggers by and seeing the fallen couple he knocks on the door.

"What do you want?" demands Madam,

He replies slowly "I just wanted to let you know your sign's fallen down."

★ ★ ★

A young man, out on his first night in Florence, walked up to a young girl on the street corner and asked "Do you understand English?"

"A leetle bit," she replied.

"How much?" he continued.

"£30."

★ ★ ★

A stranger in town, the man goes to a nightclub to find some action and spots a stunning redhead at the end of the bar, talking to a smug-looking man. As he watches, the man passes her some money and they disappear.

"Hey mate," he calls to the barman."What's the story on that redhead who was standing at the end of the bar just now?"

"Forget it," replies the barman, "she's a high class pro, and she's well out of your league."

Now the stranger's been on the rigs for several months so he's feeling quite rich. The next night he returns to the bar and sees the redhead standing in the same place but this time, she's on her own. He saunters over to her and smiles.

"What's it to be?" she asks.

"What's on offer," he replies.

"Well, I can give you a hand job for £100."

"What!" he exclaims, "you must be joking."

"Look wise guy," she says. "See this club and the casino. They're both mine. Bought by the money I made on hand jobs. That's how good they are."

So the man agrees and it's the best experience he's ever had. The next night he's back looking for more.

"It was bloody fantastic," he tells her. "What else is on offer?"

"I do a blow job for £300."

"£300!" he gasps.

"You see that Lotus Elan out there," she says pointing. "That's just one of three cars I've bought from doing blow jobs. It's the best ever."

So he eagerly pays the money and off they go. The man has an ecstatic experience and spends the whole of the next day recovering. Then he's straight back down the club, panting for more.

"I've got to have some pussy," he tells her. She looks at him sadly and beckons him outside.

"You see that," she says, pointing to a 5* hotel, across the street.

"I don't believe it," he replies astonished. "Is that yours too?"

"It would be, if I had a pussy," she replies.

★ ★ ★

115

Old Henry came across his son's bank book and inside saw details of his recent spending. It read 'Cute Carol £40, Sugarplum £45 and Lucious Lil £35.'

"Now look here son," said Henry, "if you must pay for it, at least get a better bargain and secondly, be a little more discreet when writing it down in your bank book. You enjoy golf, refer to it in those terms."

Some weeks later, Henry looked at his son's book again and was pleased to see he had taken his advice. The entries read 'green fees £20', 'green fees £25' and green fees £30.' However his satisfaction turned to shame when a fourth entry read 'repairs to putt £200'.

★ ★ ★

"No madam," insisted Jack to the owner of the brothel, "if I can't have Poppet, I won't have anyone."
"But sir, we have lots of lovely girls, what's Poppet got that the others haven't?"
"Patience," he replied.

★ ★ ★

Malcolm had been told by his mate to pop down the local brothel and insist on seeing Sugar.

"She'll do things to you that you'll remember for ever," he said.

So Malcolm did as his mate suggested, and ended up in Room 4 with the delightful Sugar. She stripped him bare, caressed his todger and then proceeded to cover it in syrup, sprinkle over some chopped walnuts, top this with cream and pour over some raspberry sauce. He lay there astonished.

"Now my darling, I will suck this off," she purred.

"Oh no you're not," he replied quickly. "You leave it alone, it looks so good, I'm going to suck it off myself."

★ ★ ★

Two drunks picked up a couple of prostitutes and took them down the local sleazy hotel. In no time at all, Tommy was well into the rhythm when his mate Al, rushed into the room. "Hey Tom, do you mind swapping, the one I've got is my sister."

★ ★ ★

It was the first time that the Bishop had visited the small town, and arrangements and celebrations had been planned for weeks. On his arrival, a young journalist squeezed his way to the front of the thronging crowds and called out to him.

"Your Worship, what about the brothels?"

The Bishop looked surprised and replied, "Are there any brothels here?"

The following day the headline in the newspaper read

"First words spoken by Bishop: Are there any brothels here?"

★ ★ ★

"Hello darling," said the cocky young man going up to the girl at the bar.

"What do you do then?"

She replied coldly, "I put a stocking on my right leg, then a stocking on my left leg, and between the two, I make a living."

★ ★ ★

The female lay-preacher went down to the local whorehouse to preach to the girls and try to persuade them to turn their backs on whoring and embrace the Lord.

She began "At one time you would have found me in the arms of soldiers, sailors and airmen but now I love the Lord..."

"Way to go, Sister," interrupted a woman from the back, "fuck 'em all."

★ ★ ★

A man went to a brothel and paid £200 for a session with Cindy. Unfortunately, she suffered a fatal stroke half-way through and collapsed on to the floor. The man rushed from the room yelling for the Madam.

"It's Cindy," he gasped, "she's died on me."

"Now calm down," said the Madam, "she hadn't been feeling well, it's not your fault. I'll call the doctor."

"What the hell for," he screamed, "I can't fuck the doctor."

★ ★ ★

The police raid the local brothel and line the girls up in the street, ready to take them down to the local nick. As they're standing there, an old woman approaches and asks what's going on.

"Waiting for our ice lollies," replies one of the girls cheekily.

Not realising she's being made fun of, the old woman takes her place at the end of the queue.

After a few minutes, the copper walks down the line of girls, making a note of their names. When he gets to the old woman he remarks

"Blimey, aren't you a bit old for this?"

"No, I am not," says the old woman angrily. "I may not have any teeth, but I can still suck."

★ ★ ★

A country priest was visiting a convent in the rough area of a big city. Not used to the transport system, he got off two stops too early so he walked the rest of the way. It wasn't long before a woman approached him and sidling up, she whispered in his ear

"Come on sir, only £10 for a blow job."

He smiled at her, shook his head and continued on his way. Soon, another woman approached, offered him a similar price, but he shook his head and walked on. By the time he reached the convent, he had been stopped more than five times. He went through the gate and spotted a young nun cleaning the windows.

"Hello Sister," he said. "I wonder if you could tell me... what is a blow job?"
"£10," she replied immediately. "That's the going rate around here."

★ ★ ★

Brian went along to the nightclub for an interview as a bouncer. "You'll do nicely," said the owner. "The pay's £120 per week, but we do throw in a few extras. Upstairs, is Madame Ruby's whorehouse and after work each night, the staff are allowed to have one of the girls for free."

"Paradise," thought Brian as he eagerly accepted the job.

The following Monday, he started work and after his shift went upstairs and was told to visit Mandy. There she sat, in a revealing nurse's uniform, and he couldn't wait to get started. However, all she did was toss him off, nothing more. The next night he tried Lindy but again, to his disappointment, she just tossed him off. And that's what happened all week. After his seven-day stint, the owner asked him how it was going.

"Okay," he said. "I'm a bit disappointed with the girls. All they do is toss me off."

"Ah, but you must remember Brian, we work a week in hand here."

★ ★ ★

A businessman and his wife were travelling up to London together, he was attending a meeting while she was going shopping. They arranged to meet up afterwards for lunch in

a restaurant just off Oxford Street. As it happens, the meeting had to be cut short and the businessman found he had over an hour to kill. He sauntered into Mayfair, where he spotted a prostitute standing on the street corner. On the spur of the moment, he went up to her and said

"How much will it cost me for half an hour?"

"Seventy five," she replied.

"Oh no! That's far too expensive. I've only got £20!" he exclaimed and walked away. Later, he met his wife in the restaurant and as they were sitting down to lunch, the prostitute walked in on the arm of an old man. He looked at her in embarrassment as she passed the table and winked at him. Then, she bent down and whispered in his ear

"See what you get when you've only got £20!"

★ ★ ★

A seedy looking bloke goes to a brothel and pays for a night with one of the girls. In the morning, he wakes up, looks in the mirror and groans.

"Oh shit, I feel lousy," he moans. "I hope you haven't got AIDS?"

"Course I ain't," she replied.

"Well thank goodness for that. I wouldn't want AIDS again."

★ ★ ★

A rich, but slightly mad old man arranged for a prostitute to come round to his house at 8 o'clock in the evening. When a beautiful curvaceous blonde arrived at the door, she asked him what he would like and he told her he wanted a bath. So she prepared the bath, he stripped off and got in.

"Now, what would you like?" she asked.

"I'd like some thunder," he said, "please bang your fist against the door."

So she did that and after a few minutes asked him again "What would you like?"

"Lightning," he replied. "Lots of lightning, please switch the light on and off."

She did this and he squealed with pleasure.

"Great!" he enthused. "Now I want waves, stormy waves."

So she leant over the bath and made waves with her hands.

By this time, the girl had been there over an hour and was getting very bored.

"Come on," she coaxed. "Don't you want some sex?"

"What!" he exclaimed. "In this weather? You must be joking."

★ ★ ★

Bob had been away at sea for six months and was desperate for a woman. As soon as he came ashore, he went to the nearest whore house and demanded their best girl. Once upstairs, he immediately stripped off and jumped straight into bed.

"Okay luv," he said to the waiting brunette, "I hope you've eaten recently."

"Yes, I have. But why?"

"'Cos you won't get another chance for the next two days," he replied.

★ ★ ★

Did you hear about the two prostitutes who went past a hairdresser's without noticing, but could smell singed hair. One said to the other
"Slow down a bit Lil, I think we're walking too fast."

★ ★ ★

A man approached the girl on the street corner and asked how much she cost.
"£20 behind the council flats or £100 for a night in an hotel."
"Okay," he said, and handed her £100.
"Oh great," she said, "it's such a bloody cold night, it'll be nice to be indoors."

★ ★ ★

A prostitute was knocked over by a car and as she lay there moaning, a young man went over to help.
"Are you all right?" he asked.
"I'm not sure," she replied. "I feel a bit dizzy."
"Well how many fingers am I holding up?"
"Oh no," she cried. "I'm paralysed as well."

★ ★ ★

MEET THE GRIM REAPER

The beautiful young girl was sitting on the park bench, crying her eyes out. When Matthew saw her unhappiness, he went over and sat down, asking what was wrong.

"Everything," she wailed. "I've just lost my job so I can't pay the mortgage and I'm going to be evicted. Then this morning I discovered I had a fatal hereditary disease which means I'll die in middle age."

"Oh dear," he said kindly, "why don't I try to cheer you up. How about coming out to dinner with me on Friday night?"

"I can't," she sniffed, "I'm going to kill myself on Friday night."

"Well all right then. How about Thursday night instead?"

★ ★ ★

"Please come in and sit down Mr. Morton," said the doctor, looking grave. "I'm afraid your test results have come back and it's very bad news. You only have a year to live."

Mr. Morton put his head in his hands and gasped.

"Oh no, oh no, what shall I do?"

"Well if I were you," replied the doctor, "I'd move out into the country, to a very quiet place, and marry an ugly, nagging woman. I assure you, it'll be the longest year of your life."

★ ★ ★

"It was a dreadful shock to us all," sobbed Mrs. Maggs. "Poor old dad!"

"Please don't upset yourself too much," comforted the vicar, "we'll make sure he has a memorable send-off. How old was he, by the way?"

"98," she replied.

"98!" exclaimed the vicar, "so why were you all so shocked?"

"We didn't know he had a bad heart till he went bungee jumping yesterday."

★ ★ ★

The funeral was over and the distraught man was sobbing his heart out at the graveside.

"Come on Jack," said his mate, trying to comfort him. "She was a great wife, but don't despair. You're still young enough to love again and in time you'll meet someone else."

"Maybe," replied Jack, "but who am I going to fuck tonight?"

★ ★ ★

Laying on his deathbed, the old man's eyes rested on the face of his sorrowful wife.

"Dear Agnes," he rasped, "we've been through a lot together. When I was just 20 my parents were killed in a car accident, and you were there for me. Then we had the terrible floods of '64 when we lost all our possessions and you helped me through it.

Now I've caught this fatal disease and here you are by my side. Do you know," he continued with a spark of anger, "I'm beginning to think you're fucking bad luck for me!"

★ ★ ★

"Hello children," said the new teacher. "Let's get to know each other better. Tell me what your fathers do for a living."
"My dad's a greengrocer," said Matthew.
"Mine's a doctor," said Jane.
"My dad works in an office," said Becky.
"And what about your father, Simon?"
"My dad's dead, miss," came the reply.
"Oh dear. What did he do before he died?"
"He grabbed his chest, groaned a lot and then fell onto the floor."

★ ★ ★

As the wife watched her husband's coffin disappear into the ground, she turned to her friend and said
"You know, Ethel, I blame myself for his death."
"Oh why?"
"Because I shot him," she replied.

★ ★ ★

"I'm sorry to bother you at this time," said the funeral director, "but your late husband died with an erection and we can't close the coffin lid. Would you mind if we cut it off and laid it beside him with the flowers?"

"No, I have a better idea," replied the widow. "Cut it off and shove it up his arse... That's what he did to me when he gave me flowers."

★ ★ ★

A 'diddle' of antique dealers are tragically killed in a plane crash and the group of 10 find themselves outside the Pearly Gates.

"Mmmm," said St Peter, scratching his head, "we don't usually let in such a lot of antique dealers at the same time. I'll have to go and ask God."

St Peter went off and found God, hard at work in his office.

"There's a group of antique dealers at the gates, shall we let them in?" he asked.

"Just this once," replied God, "if there's so many of them, they'll be too bothered about each other to cause havoc anywhere else."

St Peter went back to the entrance but returned moments later in a panic.

"They've gone!" he exclaimed breathlessly.

"What? The antique dealers?"

"No," replied Peter, "the Pearly Gates."

★ ★ ★

Arthur was lying on his deathbed, his wife had been told he only had days to live. As she sat with him on one of his last evenings, he whispered to her, "Oh Rose, now that my life is coming to an end, would you do one last thing for me. It's something that's never happened throughout our married life so please, as a last request, will you give me a blow job?" Shocked, but caught up in the emotion, Rose agreed and did it there and then. The next day, Arthur seemed slightly better and this improvement continued throughout the week until he started to sit up in bed and take food. The doctors hailed it as a miraculous recovery. Rose just sat there and cried.

"What's wrong?" asked the doctor anxiously, "your husband is going to live, you should be happy."

"I was just thinking," she sobbed. "I could have saved my handsome next-door neighbour."

★ ★ ★

The poor old woman had never had much to smile about in her life – poverty, a drunken womanising husband and two wayward kids. But she finally made it to heaven and had only been there a week when she spotted her husband who had died some years previously. There he was, a barrel of whisky at his side and a beautiful blonde on his knee.

"I can't believe it," she gasped. When a passing angel saw her distress, he asked her what was wrong.

"I've just seen my husband," she replied. "He was a real bastard on earth but look at the way he's been rewarded!" she exclaimed. The angel replied gently

"It's not what you think. That's his punishment. You see the barrel of whisky has a hole in it and the woman hasn't."

For the first time in many years, the old woman smiled.

★ ★ ★

Geoffrey was shocked to discover that his older sister had died while being serviced by two young studs. He'd never known much about his sister's secret life but the thought of it becoming public news filled him with horror.

"Oh the shame!" he cried, "the family will be tainted for ever!"

"Not to worry," said the coroner's office, "it's not the first time we've had to deal with a delicate situation like this. Even though your sister was... er... busy at the time, it was a natural death. Her heart just gave out. We'll issue our usual statement for circumstances like this."

"Oh? What's that."

"She died happily at the stroke of two."

★ ★ ★

"Number 11, legs eleven," shouted the bingo caller.

"Bingo!" came the reply, and as the balls were set up for the next game, the caller recognised old Flo sitting miserably in the corner. He walked over and said

"Hello Flo. What's up. You've got a face like a wet weekend."

"Hello Ron," she replied. "My husband died three days ago."

"Oh, I'm so sorry," he said. "So have you come here on your own?"

"I have," she replied, "and the worst thing is that no one can pick me up till much later today, after the funeral is over."

★　★　★

MEET THE HUSBAND

I'm not saying my wife is ugly, but she has to sneak up on her glass to get a drink.

★ ★ ★

"Doctor, doctor. It's the wife. She's having trouble with her eyesight," said the agitated husband.
"Really?" replied the doctor, "in what way?"
"She keeps having visions of a pearl necklace."

★ ★ ★

Derek was so frustrated. Every night his wife refused sex until one day his anger got the better of him. He arrived home with a present, wrapped up in shiny paper.

"This is for you," he said.

His wife was surprised.

"For me, what is it?"

"Open it and see," he said.

Unwrapping the paper, she discovered a basket with four little kittens inside.

"Oh! They're adorable," she cried, "but why?"

"I thought they could carry the coffin of your dead pussy," he replied sharply.

★ ★ ★

A man walked into his home and yelled at his wife.

"Mildred, I've just discovered our marriage is illegal."

"How come?" she replied.

"Your father didn't have a licence for that shotgun."

★ ★ ★

"My wife caught a Peeping Tom last night just as she was getting ready for bed. Phew! She was so angry, she beat him black and blue."

"I'm not surprised. It's a dreadful feeling to think that someone was watching you as you got undressed."

"No, no, it wasn't that. It was when he tried to close the curtains."

★ ★ ★

There was a couple who liked to party every night. One day, on the way home from work, having spent his last £5 in the pub at lunchtime, the husband passed an old beggar and threw him his last few coins. Lo and behold, the beggar turned into a genie and granted the man one wish for being so kind to him.

"I could do with a drink," said the man.

"Well I've got just the answer," replied the genie. "Every time you need a pee, you'll piss 5mls of brandy. It'll be the best you've ever had."

"Get away with you," laughed the man and continued home. However the incident stayed in the man's head and the next time he went to the loo, he peed into a small container. It smelled like brandy. He sipped it – and it tasted wonderful.

"Hey, Marge, get a load of this," he yelled to his wife and for the rest of the evening they drank to their heart's content. Every day that week, he'd come home, Marge would get the glasses out and away they'd go.

Then on Saturday night the husband turned to his wife and said, "Marge, bring me one glass please."

She did as she was asked and he peed into it.

"Why only one glass tonight?" she asked puzzled.

"Well my love," he replied, "I thought you could drink straight from the bottle."

★ ★ ★

"Colin," she whispered, nudging him in the ribs to wake him up. "I can hear noises downstairs, I think we've got burglars. Go and see."

But Colin refused to move.

"What's happened to you," she hissed. "You were brave when you married me."

"I know," he replied, "that's what all my friends said."

★ ★ ★

"Look at this!" exclaimed the angry husband to his wife, "the bank has returned the cheque you wrote last week."

"Oh great," she replied. "I wonder what I'll spend it on next."

★ ★ ★

Why are men who have pierced ears ready for marriage?
They've known pain and bought jewellery.

★ ★ ★

A man sat staring sadly into his pint of beer.

"Hello Jack, what's wrong?" asked his mate, sitting down next to him.

"It's the wife," he replied. "We had a terrible fight last night and she came crawling over to me on her hands and knees..."

"Oh Lord! That's awful," interrupted his friend.

"...and she said 'come out from under that bed or I'll put you in hospital'."

★ ★ ★

"Dad, dad," said his son excitedly. "I've done it. I've got a part in the new play."

"Well done lad, what is it?"

"I play an old man who's been married for 35 years."

"That's a promising start. Next time you might get a speaking part."

★ ★ ★

Percy arrived home in the early hours of the morning, drunk as a skunk. Not wanting to face his wife's wrath, he very quietly tiptoed up the stairs but just as he got to the top, the cuckoo clock cuckooed once.

Percy cursed and thinking quickly cuckooed another eleven times, knowing his wife would have woken up at the sound of the clock.

"You're very late," said his wife, sitting up in bed.

"Oh, perhaps a little," he replied, "it's only 12 o'clock." With that he slipped into bed and was just closing his eyes when she replied.

"Mmm, by the way, you'd better take the clock in for repairs tomorrow. It cuckooed once, said 'Oh fuck', belched, farted and then cuckooed another eleven times."

★ ★ ★

Two men, both sporting black eyes, found themselves travelling in the same railway carriage.

"Excuse me," said the first man. "I can't help but notice we've both got black eyes. How did you get yours?"

"I just said something by accident," replied the other. "I went to the counter to buy my ticket and there was the most gorgeous blonde you've ever seen. Not only that, she had the biggest breasts ever. I was so overcome, instead of asking for a ticket to Pittsburgh, I asked for a picket to Tittsburgh. Boom! She threw me a right."

"Yeah, I can understand that," mused the first man. "I got mine the same way, by saying something accidentally. It was at breakfast this morning when my wife asked me to pass the marmalade. I replied 'Get it yourself, you hard-bitten bitch, you've ruined my fucking life.'"

★ ★ ★

A man walked into a chemist and asked for a large-size condom. He then went next door to the sweet shop and asked for the condom to be filled with four scoops of ice cream.
The shopkeeper was dumbfounded.
"Excuse me, sir, I have to ask. Why are you filling this with ice cream?"
"Well, it's my wife's birthday," he replied. "Over the years I've bought her many, many things from jewels and furs to exotic holidays to labour saving devices such as a washing machine, microwave, dishwasher and every conceivable kitchen gadget."
"So?" puzzled the shopkeeper.
"So, tonight, I'm going to give her a deep freeze."

★ ★ ★

Geoffrey found his host in the library.
"I'm very sorry," he began. "I just walked into the bathroom to find your wife having a bath. Do forgive me."
His host looked up sadly and replied "Bloody skinny bugger, isn't she?"

★ ★ ★

A man and his wife went on safari and having lost the rest of the sightseeing party, they found themselves alone in the jungle. Suddenly the wife screamed as they were confronted by a huge gorilla. He grabbed her by the arse and began tearing her clothes off.
"Help, Fred, help me, what shall I do?" she yelled.
"Tell him you've got a headache and you're too tired," he replied.

★ ★ ★

Over a few pints of beer, two men were so engrossed in their conversation that they didn't notice the time. Suddenly last orders were called and the first man cursed out loud.
"Bugger! That's me for the cold-shoulder treatment, I promised the wife I'd be home early."
He looked glumly into his pint and continued, "I just can't win. Whenever I go out I make sure none of the doors squeak, I oil the garden gate, I move anything I might trip over in the dark and then when I get home, I take my shoes off before going upstairs, undress in the bathroom and slip very quietly into bed. And it never bloody works! She still turns over and shouts 'Where have you been until this time of night?'"
"No mate," said the second man, "you're doing it all wrong. When I get home late at night, I swing the garden gate backwards and forwards to make as much squeaking noise as possible. Then I slam the front door, turn on all the lights, and stomp up the stairs into the bedroom. I jump into bed and give the wife a good

nudge in the ribs and say 'How about it then luv?' and you can bet you've never seen a woman sleep so deeply."

★ ★ ★

"It's no good," cried the downtrodden husband. "I can't go on. I'm off to join the Foreign Legion."
"Very well," retorted the wife, "but don't let me find you trailing sand all over my nice new carpet when you get back."

★ ★ ★

Walter was hammering away in the garden when George popped his head up over the wall.

"Fancy a pint, Walt?" he asked.

"No, I can't," replied Walter sadly. "The wife's ill in bed, so I've got to look after her."

As if on cue, they heard terrible noises coming from the house.

"Is that her coughing?" asked George.

"Don't be a daft prat," replied Walter. "She couldn't get inside this. It's too small. It's going to be a new kennel for the dog."

★ ★ ★

As John got undressed, ready for bed, his wife turned to him in alarm.
"John, why have you got that cork sticking out of your bum?"
"Oh no," groaned John, putting his head in his hands.

"If only I hadn't gone to the tip this morning," he continued. "While I was there, I spotted this bottle glinting in the sun. I rubbed off the mud to get a closer look and a genie appeared. He said he'd grant me anything I wanted."

"Well, what do you say?" asked his wife impatiently.

"I said, no shit."

★ ★ ★

Two couples went away on holiday together, stopping in two caravans on the south coast. Because the men tended to stay out late boozing, it was decided that the women would share one caravan and the men would share the other.

On the third night, Jack woke up suddenly and exclaimed "Bloody hell, I've got such a big one on me tonight. The best ever. I'll have to go and see the wife."

"Do you want me to come with you?" asked Bob.

"Of course not. Why do you ask?"

"Because it's my dick you're holding."

★ ★ ★

Three husbands were discussing what they were going to buy their wives for Christmas.

"I'm getting Doreen one of those new food blenders, she's always wanted one," said Steve.

"I'm getting my wife a gold chain and matching earrings," said Chris.

The third man remained strangely quiet.
"Come on Jeff," urged the other two, "what are you going to
get your wife?
"My bloody wife is so hard to please," he complained.
"I'm going to get her a real leather handbag and a dildo.
Then if she doesn't like the bag, she can go fuck herself!"
he said bitterly.

★ ★ ★

A man went to the doctor's complaining that he could no longer
satisfy his wife's sexual desires.
"We'll soon put that right," said the doctor, "take two of these
pills before bed and you'll see a great difference."
That night, the man got out his bottle of pills and took two. Then
he thought to himself "the wife's got a good sexual appetite" so
he took two more. Then he thought "I'll take a couple to keep my
energy up and a couple for luck!"
What an evening! The man had never felt so virile. He took his
wife to bed and satisfied her time and time again until she fell
into an exhausted sleep. Around three in the morning, she woke
up to find her husband wasn't in bed. So she went in search of
him. At the bottom of the stairs, she found the cat, purring
contentedly, then in the kitchen she found the dog wagging its tail
enthusiastically. But there was no sign of her husband. Suddenly,
she heard a noise from the shed and when she peered through the
door, there was her husband with his todger in a vice and some
sandpaper in his hand.

"George, what are you doing?" she gasped.

"Listen Doris, you're satisfied, the cat's satisfied, the dog's satisfied, so I'm not going to leave the budgie out of this!"

★ ★ ★

Fed up with his wife's lack of interest, Jack got into bed and handed her a glass of water and a couple of Paracetamol.
"Here you are darling, that's for your headache."
"But I haven't got a headache."
"Good, then how about a shag?"

★ ★ ★

The husband was standing on the crowded platform when he thought he saw his wife amongst the crowd. He pushed his way through the people, came up behind her and gave her a big hug and a lip-smacking kiss on the neck. Alas, as the woman turned round, he realised it wasn't his wife.

"Oh no, I'm so sorry," he said blushing profusely.

"It's just that your head looks like my wife's behind," he stammered.

★ ★ ★

MEET THE KIDS

A little girl was watching her father take a shower . She asked him what his testicles were called.

"They're my plums," he replied.

A little later she told her mother what he had said.

Mum retorted "And did he tell you about the dead branch they are hanging off?"

★ ★ ★

"Great news dad," said the son who had been minding his father's shop.

"You remember that checked suit in bright green and yellow... The one you thought you'd be stuck with forever? Well, I've sold it, and at the asking price."

"Well, that's fantastic," replied the dad, very impressed. "Well done, I think you deserve a bonus for that. By the way, why have you got a bandage on your hand?"

"Oh that's where his guide dog bit me."

★ ★ ★

The pretty young teacher had been form tutor of the Year 8 boys for half a term. Over the past few days she had noticed that one of her pupils had become distracted. Instead of getting on with his work, he would just gaze into space. Eventually she asked him to stay behind so she could have a quiet word.

"Billy, you used to be such a hard worker but something's happened to change all this. What is it?"

"I'm in love, miss," he replied.

She smiled, sympathetically. "And who is it?"

"It's you miss. All I can think about is you."

The young teacher looked embarrassed.

"Oh Billy," she said softly, "sometimes life isn't that simple. I, too, have dreams. I dream of getting married but I don't want a child..."

"Oh that's all right miss," he interrupted, "I've brought a condom."

★ ★ ★

"Cynthia," said her governess angrily, "it didn't look good letting that strange man kiss you in front of the rest of the class."

"Well actually, miss, it was better than it looked."

★ ★ ★

The student teacher was sitting in on a religious education lesson in class 4B. Suddenly, the teacher turned to her and said

"Miss Lustleigh, will you tell the class the name of the first man."

"Well, I could," she replied coyly, "but I promised we'd keep it a secret."

★ ★ ★

The woman was walking down the street when she saw a young boy standing on the corner, drinking from a can of beer and smoking a cigarette.

"Why, this is disgraceful!" she exclaimed. "You should be in school."

"Piss off," he replied, "I'm only four years old."

★ ★ ★

"Mummy, mummy!" cried the little boy, when he saw his mother in the shower. "What's that hair?" he said, pointing to her pubes. Mum blushed and replied

"Well, that's my sponge."

"Oh I understand now," said the little boy, "'cos I saw the housemaid washing daddy's face with hers yesterday."

★ ★ ★

Two little babies were talking to each other at the clinic.

"I only get milk from the bottle," complained the first one.

"You're lucky, breast milk is supposed to be a lot better."

"Not if you have to share it with a man who smokes a pipe," retorted the second.

★ ★ ★

A little boy started school but was causing a great deal of trouble for the teachers. Each lunch-time, he would be taken to the dining room for dinner but once there, he would refuse to sit down.

"Bollocks!" he would shout at the top of his voice.

When he repeated this behaviour, the following day, he was reprimanded but it didn't have much effect. Again, he shouted "Bollocks!"

At the end of the week, his parents were contacted and told about his behaviour.

"Well, if that's how the little bugger acts, bollocks to him. Don't give him any dinner," replied dad.

★ ★ ★

The little girl ran crying to her teacher.

"Please miss, can I have some cider? I've hurt my finger."

"But why do you want some cider?" asked the teacher.

"Because I heard my sister say that whenever she gets a prick in her hand, she always puts it in cider."

★ ★ ★

A little boy was playing pirates in the park when the Mayoress happened to walk by.

"Hello Tommy," she said. "What are you up to?"

"I'm the Captain and me and my men are going to fight all the enemy ships," he said, brandishing his cardboard cutlass and putting on his eye patch.

"So where are the buccaneers?" she asked, looking round.

"Under my buck'on hat of course," he replied.

★ ★ ★

"Mummy, mummy, are birds made of metal?"

"Goodness me, that's an odd question," replied mum. "Why do you ask?"

"Because I've just heard dad on the telephone saying he would like to screw the arse off the bird next door."

★ ★ ★

"Hey, mummy, I know how babies are made," said the little girl. "I saw daddy put his willy in your mouth last night."

"No darling, you've got that wrong. That's how I get my fur coat."

★ ★ ★

"All right class," said the teacher. "Quieten down and each of you tell me in turn what would you like your body to be made of, if you had the choice."

"I'd like my body to be made of £10 notes," said one little girl, "then I could take some off and buy a car."

"Okay," replied the teacher, "who's next?"

"I would like my body to be made of gold," said Josie, "then I'd only need a little bit of it to buy two cars."

"Thank you Josie. How about you, Ben?"

"I'd have my body made out of pubic hair, miss."

"Good gracious!" she exclaimed. "Whatever for?"

"Well my big sister's only got a small patch, but there's always plenty of cars parked outside our house!"

★ ★ ★

The English schoolmistress was testing her children's knowledge of famous quotes.

"All right class," she said, "whoever gives me the right answer can go home an hour early from school."

She stood before them and began.

"The first quote is 'Tis better to have loved and lost than never to have loved at all.'"

A hand went up immediately.

"Please miss," said Beth "that's Alfred Lord Tennyson."

"Very good," beamed the teacher. "You may go."

Then she read out a second quote. "Every dog has it's day, and I have had mine."

Mary put her hand up. "Bernard Shaw, miss."

"Well done, off you go."

"Bloody girls, I wish they'd shut up," murmured Tommy, from the back.

"Who said that," demanded the teacher looking round.

"President Clinton," said Tommy quickly, and before she could answer he'd dashed from the class.

★ ★ ★

A boy went off to college and within the first month he'd spent all his grant. So he thought up a great scam. He rang his dad and said "Dad, this is an amazing place. They do research into the most extraordinary things. Do you know, they've told me they can make our parrot think and talk for himself. Can I bring him up here? I'll need £1,000 towards the research."

His dad was very impressed.

"Okay son, fancy that, we could make a fortune out of it."

The bird and the money arrived and of course, he blew the lot within a month. So he rang his dad again.

"It's even better than I thought. They reckon they can teach him to read as well. But I'll need another £2,000."

The money arrived, and the money was spent.

Then came the day that the boy had to return home and take the parrot with him. His trick would be discovered and he dreaded his father's reaction so he strangled the parrot and returned alone.

"Hello son," said dad excitedly, as he met him at the station. "Where's the bird then?"

"Dad, brace yourself for some bad news. We were on the way to catch our train when the parrot turned to me and said "It'll be good to see home again. I wonder if your dad is still fucking the woman across the street!"

"I hope you rung the lying bugger's neck," cried his dad.

★ ★ ★

Walking through the village, the local vicar spotted young Billy with a herd of bullocks.

"There's a fine looking herd," he remarked.

"Yeah," replied Billy. "Dad made 'em."

"Oh no son," said the vicar shaking his head, "God made those bullocks."

"No," argued Billy. "God made them bulls, dad made them bullocks."

★ ★ ★

A catholic boy and a C of E boy were trying to score points off each other.
"My priest knows more than your vicar," said the first little boy.
"That's because you tell him everything," replied the second.

★ ★ ★

The baby was so ugly when it was born that the doctor drew a circle round its mouth in case they fed it's backside by mistake.

★ ★ ★

"Okay kids," said dad, returning home from work. "My boss gave me a box of chocolates today so I think it ought to go to the person who always does what mummy says and never answers her back."
"Oh dad," wailed the four children, "that's not fair, you know that's you!"

★ ★ ★

"Mummy, mummy," said the little girl, "when you die and go to heaven, does God pull you up by the legs?"
"Oh no," replied mum puzzled, "why do you ask?"
"After you'd gone shopping yesterday I saw the lady from next door. She was lying in her garden shouting "Oh God, I'm

coming, I'm coming" and I think she would have gone, mummy, if daddy hadn't been holding her down."

★ ★ ★

Two streetwise kids were walking to school when one said to the other, "Guess what, I found a condom on the patio." The other replied, "So what's a patio then?"

★ ★ ★

It was the end of year exams and an examiner from another school had come in to adjudicate.

"You will start when I ring this bell," he told the class, "and you will finish when I ring it a second time. Anyone found writing after that will be disqualified. At the end, please bring your papers up and then you are free to leave."

The class started on the bell and Jake began writing feverishly. His concluding sentence was all important but it meant he finished a couple of seconds after the bell. When he got up to hand his paper in, the strict adjudicator informed him he was disqualified

"Do you know who I am?" demanded Jake.

"No," replied the adjudicator frostily.

"Are you sure?"

"Absolutely."

"Good," replied Jake as he swiftly put his paper into the middle of the stack and ran out of the door.

★ ★ ★

Derek Cox was looking for his son. He'd been round most of the usual haunts and decided to try the barber's on the way home.

"Excuse me," he said, putting his head round the door. "Bob Cox in here?"

"No, sir, I'm afraid not. We only do haircuts and shaves."

★ ★ ★

MEET THE LAWMAN

The little man was found guilty of fraud and sentenced to three years in prison. When he arrived, he was put in a cell with a huge gorilla of a man who was doing thirty years for murder. The "gorilla" looked at the little man with relish and said

"My name's Digger and what I need to know is whether you're going to be the husband or the wife."

Choosing what he thought was the lesser of two evils, the terrified man chose husband.

"Good," snarled the big man. "Now get down on your knees and suck your wife's dick."

★ ★ ★

"And where do you think you're going at this time of night?" the police officer asked the staggering drunk.

"To a lecture," he replied.

"Come off it. It's one o'clock in the morning. Who'd be giving a lecture at this late hour?"

"My wife."

★ ★ ★

The divorce judge looked down at the hapless couple and shook his head in bafflement.

"I just don't understand," he said. "Here you are, a young prosperous couple with two beautiful children and yet you say the marriage has failed. Why is that?"

"It's the sex," cried the woman. "It's a disaster."

The judge looked down at his notes and said

"I see here, that your husband is in the SAS. Surely that would make him very athletic, full of get up and go?"

"But that's just the trouble" she replied, sadly. "He may be fit enough, but they taught him how to get in and out of sticky situations without anyone noticing."

★ ★ ★

Did you hear about the humiliated flasher?
His case was heard in the Small Claims Court.

★ ★ ★

An explosion at the chemical factory meant that everyone in a five-mile radius had to be evacuated. They were sent to community centres to spend the night on an assortment of mattresses. Around midnight, the local police checked out the people and one officer said

"Are there any pregnant women here?"

"Have a heart," a woman replied, "we've only been here a few minutes."

★ ★ ★

The policeman was on duty in the red light district and as he shone his torch up an alley, he saw Brenda. She was standing there with her blouse undone and her knickers round her ankles, eating a packet of crisps.

"Come on Brenda, what's going on?" he said.

"Oh hello Sarge," she replied cheekily, then looking round added, "Blimey, has he gone?"

★ ★ ★

As the policeman walked down Lovers Lane he spotted a car rocking from side to side.

"What's going on here?" he demanded, shining his torch through the window.

"Oh nothing much," said the boy hastily, "er... just a little necking."

"Well, in that case, put your neck back in your trousers and get out of here."

★ ★ ★

The Managing Director was up in court on a charge of sexual harassment.

"Now, my dear," said the judge to the tearful young girl. "If you could just tell us in your own words what this man said to you."

"Oh no, I couldn't," she stammered. "It's too embarrassing."

So it was decided she would write down the words for all to read. After the judge had read the note, he passed it to the foreman of the jury who then passed it to his colleagues. At the end of the line, it was passed to an old spinster who had momentarily dozed off. She picked up the note and read the words

"Meet me in the basement and leave your knickers behind." She looked up, nodded, grinned at the Foreman and put the note in her pocket.

★ ★ ★

A young police officer was being shown his new beat. After a couple of hours driving around, he and his sergeant stopped for coffee at a local café. They'd just finished when in walked a stunning woman. Her figure was like an hourglass and left very little to the imagination.

"Wow!" whistled the copper under his breath, "who's that Sarge? I've never seen anything like her."

"They call her 999."

"Yeah? Why?"

"Every time she calls, a copper comes."

★ ★ ★

"Maurice Highton, you are up before this court for shooting your wife. Do you have anything to say?"

"Yes M'lud," he replied, "She called me a dreadful lover."

"And you killed her for saying that?"

"No," he answered, angrily. "I killed her for knowing the difference."

★ ★ ★

"Mr. Merino, you are up before this court for the serious crime of assault against one of your neighbours. Before I pass sentence, can you tell me the circumstances behind this attack?"

"Yes, Your Honour," replied the defendant.

"That low down skunk called my wife an ugly old bag. He said she had a moustache bigger than his, bad breath and legs like tree trunks. I had to defend her honour."

"Mmm," mused the judge, "and is your wife here to testify on your behalf?"

"Well, the thing is, er... Will it affect your judgement if the allegations are true?" he asked.

★ ★ ★

Our town was so lawless, if you went to buy a pair of tights, they'd ask you for your head size.

★ ★ ★

"Luigi, Luigi," shouted the children as they lined up outside the ice cream van. But Luigi was nowhere to be seen. The motor was running, the music was playing but no-one was serving.

"Stand back kids," said a policeman attracted by all the noise. "What have we here?" The policeman peered inside the van and caught sight of Luigi lying on the floor. He was covered in chocolate sauce, mixed nuts and fresh cream.

"Sarge," he said, speaking into his radio. "This is PC Mann, I need some back-up at Luigi's ice-cream van on Prospect Street. It's bad news I'm afraid, Luigi's topped himself."

★ ★ ★

A policeman was patrolling the streets late one night when he spotted a car parked up a side alley. He shone his torch through the back window and saw a young couple playing Scrabble.

"What's going on here?" he demanded.

"We're just playing Scrabble," replied the boy.

"That's an odd thing to do at this time of night," he said, looking suspiciously at the girl.

"And how old are you?" he asked.

She looked up at the church clock and replied happily, "In 10 minutes time I'll be 16."

★ ★ ★

A man was caught short and so relieved himself in the bushes just as a policeman walked by.

"What the hell are you doing," he demanded angrily. "There's a public toilet just down there."

"It may be big," retorted the man, "but it's not a bloody hose pipe."

★ ★ ★

"You didn't stop at the last junction," said the policeman to the motorist. "I'll have to breathalyse you." The officer held up the bag.

"What's that?" asked the driver.

"This tells you if you've had too much to drink," he replied.

"Well I never!" he exclaimed "I'm married to one of those."

★ ★ ★

The truck driver ran a red light and was immediately picked up by the traffic cops.

"Name and place of employment, please," demanded the officer.

"Bob Wankbreak, Dyson's Mills," came the reply.

A week later the officer had to deliver notice of court proceedings, so contacted the company for verification. He rang reception and asked "Have you got a Wankbreak there?"

"You must be joking," came the reply. "It's so busy, we've hardly got time for a cup of tea."

★ ★ ★

The police car indicated for the motorist to pull up.

"Did you realise, sir, you were doing 55mph in a 30mph area," he said, pulling out his notebook. May I have your name please."

"Malenovich Salkonovichiski," came the reply.

"Okay, well just don't do it again," replied the officer, closing his book and walking away.

★ ★ ★

A man and his tiger were walking through the park when they were stopped by a policeman.

"Look, I told you yesterday to take that tiger to the zoo," said the officer.

"I did," replied the man. "Then we went to the cinema and this morning we went bowling. Now we're going to have a picnic in the park."

★ ★ ★

"I want a divorce," said the woman to her lawyer.

"And can you tell me why?" he asked.

"Because each night in bed my husband let's out this bloodcurdling scream every time he reaches a climax."

The lawyer blushed profusely and said "But er... surely that's quite normal, isn't it?"

"Not when it wakes me up every night," she retorted.

★ ★ ★

The trial was going badly for the defendant. He was charged with murder and although the body had never been found, there was enough evidence to convict him. As a last desperate effort, the defending lawyer decided to play a trick. He stood up, looked at the jury and said "Ladies and gentlemen, I have an announcement to make. In exactly 30 seconds, the person presumed murdered will walk into this courtroom."

There was stunned silence as all the jury looked towards the door, but nothing happened.

The defending lawyer continued "So members of the jury, although I made that last statement up, because you all looked at the door proves there is an element of doubt. Therefore I put it to you that you have no other course than to find the defendant not guilty."

A short while later the jury retired to consider their verdict and it was only 20 minutes before they returned.

"We find the defendant guilty," they proclaimed.

"But how can that be?" asked the lawyer. "You all looked towards the door, you must have had some doubt."

The foreman of the jury replied "That's true, we did all look towards the door. But your client didn't."

★ ★ ★

A group of firemen from the amber watch division went to Blackpool on a works' outing. They made full use of all the resort had to offer and stayed overnight in one of the seaside hotels.

Then at two in the morning, there was an awful hullabaloo and as the guests looked out of their doors, they caught sight of a naked man running down the corridor, chasing a girl who was screaming at the top of her voice. Naturally the man, who was one of the firemen, was taken to court for lewd behaviour, but it was the brilliance of his barrister that got him off without a blemish to his name. The barrister simply quoted from the service handbook which stated "A member of the fire service need not wear his uniform at all times as long as he is suitably attired for the sport in which he is involved."

★ ★ ★

On his travels abroad, a judge visited a court in a new third world developing country. His guide informed him that the court and its proceedings had been based on the English judicial system, and sure enough the judge and barristers were wearing wigs and gowns and all the proceedings were conducted in an English manner. Suddenly he was astonished to see a youth, wearing white gloves, run through the room feeling all the women's breasts. The extraordinary sight was ignored by everyone.

"Why isn't that boy expelled from the court?" demanded the visiting judge.

"But we're only following English traditions," replied the guide. "He's the Court Titter. We've read about him often in the court accounts – 'A titter ran through the crowd.'"

★ ★ ★

"Now Mr Carstairs," said the judge, "before I pass sentence, is there anything you want to say?"

"Fuck all," mumbled the defendant.

"I'm sorry, I didn't hear that," replied the judge. He looked down at the clerk and said "What did that man say?"

"'Fuck all', M'lud," came the reply.

"Really?" replied the judge. "I was sure I saw his lips move."

★ ★ ★

The court adjourned while the judge considered the appropriate sentence for an old street whore down on her luck. Unable to come to a decision, he rang his colleague.

"Jack, it's Doug here. What would you give an old, down-and-out prostitute?"

Quick as a flash the reply came "Not more than ten quid."

★ ★ ★

The shopaholic 'money-mad' woman told the judge she couldn't serve on the jury because she didn't believe in capital punishment.

"But madam," replied the judge patiently. "This is not a murder trial, it's a simple case of a husband reneging on his promise to buy his wife a new sports car."

"Okay, okay," she conceded. "Maybe there is a case for capital punishment after all."

★ ★ ★

"What's going on here?" demanded the policeman, seeing a man writhing around in agony on the ground.

"Bollocks," gasped the man. "He kicked me in the bollocks," he moaned, pointing to a man standing nearby.

"Honest, guv, it was an accident," said the other man. "How did I know he was going to turn round at the last momen?"

★ ★ ★

The judge pronounced the man guilty as charged and ordered him to be taken from the court to a place where he would face the firing squad.

As the troops escorted the prisoner on the two-mile trek to the execution area, the heavens opened and it rained furiously.

"Bloody awful weather," moaned the man. "All this bloody way, soaking wet, freezing cold, just to be shot."

"Shut up, will you," replied one of the soldiers. "At least you don't have to walk all the way back in it."

★ ★ ★

There had been so much trouble in the border settlement, that a curfew had been enforced from 10pm. Two men set out to patrol the eastern part of town and were walking down either side of the main street. Suddenly a shot rang out and the first patrolman ran over to find his partner holding out his smoking gun and a man lying dead at his feet.

"Why did you shoot him?" he asked. "There's still 20 minutes before curfew."

"Maybe," replied his partner, "but I know where this man lives and he would never have got home in time."

★ ★ ★

A man was in court for killing his wife. When he saw the jury – only two men and the rest women, he felt his chances of getting off were very slim. Now he was quite a handsome man, so in desperation he thought he would try to seduce one of the women on the jury and persuade her to drop the murder verdict to one of manslaughter. He succeeded and when the trial came to an end the following Monday, the jury left to consider their verdict. A few hours later they returned and found him guilty of manslaughter. He sighed with relief and later managed to speak to the woman to thank her for all she'd done.

"Well, it wasn't that easy," she replied. "The others wanted to acquit you."

★ ★ ★

MEET THE LOVER

"I love you very much," said the ardent young lover. "I may not have much money, like my mate Martin, I may not have a sports car or a cottage in the country like him. But I love you with all my heart and everything I have is yours."
"Very nice," she replied, preoccupied, "but just tell me a little more about Martin."

★ ★ ★

"Sweetheart," said the young man, "since I met you, I can't eat, I can't drink, in fact I can't do anything."
Thinking he was lovesick, she replied confidently
"Why's that?"
"Because I'm flat broke," came the reply.

★ ★ ★

How do you know when your girlfriend is really hot?
When you put your hand in her knickers and it feels like you're feeding a horse.

★ ★ ★

"Sir," said the young man to the girl's father, "your daughter has told me she loves me so much, she can't live without me and she wants us to get married."

"I see. So you want my permission."

"No. I want you to tell her to leave me alone."

★ ★ ★

An arrogant man loved to show-off in front of his mates. He saw this girl coming down the street and swaggered up to her.

"Hey, darling, what do you say to some ass?"

"Hello ass," she replied, walking away.

★ ★ ★

The young girl stormed back into the flat looking very angry.

"What's up with you?" asked her friend.

"It's my new boyfriend, Colin. I had to slap his face four times tonight."

"Really?!" she exclaimed, "trying it on all the time, is he?"

"No," she retorted. "The bugger keeps falling asleep."

★ ★ ★

"Darling, quick in here," said the Italian woman excitedly. She dragged him into the bedroom and began to remove his clothes. "I have discovered you can get special sprays for here," she said, pointing to her pussy. "They come in lots of different flavours – chocolate, banana, strawberry..."

He interrupted her impatiently.

"What flavour did you get?" he asked with anticipation.

"Anchovy," she replied.

★ ★ ★

"Mr Howard, your daughter is going to marry me."
"Well, that's your fault for hanging around here too much."

★ ★ ★

A public school boy fell deeply in love with the barmaid at the local pub. He desperately wanted to marry her but was afraid to take her home to ma and pa because of her working class background. He saved up all his substantial allowance and sent her off to a finishing school in Switzerland for a month's intensive course. When she returned, her whole demeanour and conversation were impeccable. He was delighted. The following day they set out for the family estate, so happy in each other's company. Suddenly, she turned to him and said

"Darling, while I was away were you blue?"

"Tut, tut," he replied. "You've only been back a day and already you're getting your tenses mixed up."

★ ★ ★

The car was parked down lovers' lane and was rocking backwards and forwards as the young couple got it together on the back seat.

171

"Oh James," she whispered passionately. "Will you love me like this when we're married?"

"You bet," he replied, "I really go for married women."

★ ★ ★

The young girl was going out on her first date and was very apprehensive.

"Don't worry," said her mum. "Just act normal, compliment him and I'm sure you'll get on fine."

So the nervous couple arrived at the disco and began dancing. Remembering what her mother had said about compliments she danced closer to him and said

"For a fat boy, you don't sweat much."

★ ★ ★

"Gloria, when did you first realise you loved me?"

"When I got upset at people saying you were ugly, fat and fucking useless."

★ ★ ★

Larry came into the pub grinning all over his face.

"What've you been up to?" asked his mate, Dave.

"Come here," said Larry, taking him to one side. "Last night, I discovered a great way to spice up the old sex life. You ought to try it. Mount your girlfriend from behind and just as you're getting comfortable, whisper in her ear 'this is the way I like it with your best mate'. Then see how long you can stay on!"

★　★　★

Wherever Troy went, he was always surrounded by girls. His handsome features, bronzed body would have the girls flocking to him. So it was with some puzzlement that when he walked into the local pub, he was left on his own. After a few minutes, he called the barman over.

"Jack, what's going on. Where's my fan club?"

"Over there," pointed Jack, "behind the pillar."

Troy sauntered over and to his astonishment, he saw a group of girls sitting round a middle-aged man of nondescript appearance.

"Hi girls," he called, thinking they hadn't seen him come in.

"Oh hi Troy," they called back, but made no move to join him. Troy went back to the bar.

"I don't understand it Jack, what's he got that I haven't?"

"No idea," replied Jack. "He doesn't come here often, but when he does, it's always the same. Like bees round a honey pot. And do you know, he hardly speaks? He just sits there, smiling, and licking his eyebrows."

★　★　★

Three women were taking tea in the Ritz and discussing their current lovers.

"Before we make love," said the rich middle class woman, "I insist he buys me a piece of jewellery and depending how much I like it, our lovemaking can be average to absolutely wild."

"Yes, yes," said the second woman who had an Italian lover. "We don't have time for all that. The only thing he says before we start is "What time will your husband be home?""

The two women turned to the third, who'd been quietly listening. She was Australian.

"So what happens before you make love?" they asked.

"Not a lot," she replied. "Bruce just says brace yourself darling."

★ ★ ★

The local headmaster had the hots for the English teacher and one night after school they found themselves alone in the gymnasium. His passion roused, they were soon entwined on the floor when a voice said

"Good evening Mr Chalmers."

"Oh... er... Good evening Mr Bates," replied the flustered headmaster to his caretaker. "I didn't hear you drive up."

"No, you wouldn't," replied the caretaker. "I don't have a car any more, I use my bike. Do you see it chained to the post?"

"Oh yes," said the headmaster, looking out of the window.

"In fact I want to sell it," continued the caretaker, "so that I can take a holiday."

"Well, I hope you do," replied the headmaster, his mind elsewhere.

"Would you like to buy it?"

"Um ... no, no thank you," said the headmaster, rearranging his clothes.

"Well that's a shame, because I shall be bumping into one of the governors tonight and I'll have to tell them about our meeting!"

"Well all right, then," sighed the headmaster, "how much?"

"£200," he replied.

"But that's ludicrous!" exclaimed the headmaster, then he remembered the threat and had to agree.

The following week, he was cycling to school when he bumped into his neighbour.

"Hello Charles, bit of an old rust bucket you have there. Pick it up from the tip, did you?"

"No, certainly not," said the headmaster peevishly. "I bought this."

"Blimey! How much?"

"£200."

"For Pete's sake, they must have seen you coming!" he exclaimed.

★ ★ ★

A couple have been courting for a few weeks when they realise they want to take their relationship further. But first, she has something to confess to him.

"Donald, darling, before we make love, I think I ought to tell you, my tits are very small. In fact, I wear falsies."

"Well, I've got something to tell you as well," he says. "I've got a cock the size of a baby."

Happy that they've been honest with each other, they go back to his place and strip off. She removes her falsies and he drops his pants.

"Oh my goodness," she gasps on seeing his manhood.

"Well, I did warn you it was like a baby," he says, "8lbs in weight."

★ ★ ★

On their first date, Harold took his girlfriend to the cinema to watch the latest James Bond movie. When they came out, he bought her a burger and then offered to walk her home. He felt pretty good. Everything was going well and he thought he might even score. When they reached her flat, she invited him in for a coffee and soon they were sitting close together on the sofa. Harold made his move. He put his hand on her knee and gently moved it up under her skirt. Suddenly, she drew away in anger and said

"Harold Morley! You're no gentleman. Don't you know it's always tits first."

★ ★ ★

"Ooh, what a big one!" she exclaimed, when he showed her his pride and glory.

"But if we have oral sex, won't I lose your respect?"

"Of course not," he replied. "Just as long as you're good at it."

★ ★ ★

The man was thrusting away energetically when she stopped him, saying
"Steve, not so hard, I've got a weak heart."
"Don't worry," he replied.
"When I get that far, I'll be more gentle."

★ ★ ★

One Sunday morning, a young couple decided to take a walk through the nearby forest. It was such a lovely day, that they stopped for a while in a clearing, one thing led to another and soon they were writhing around on the ground. Suddenly the girl cried out in pain.

"What's wrong?" asked the man, looking concerned.

"I think I've got a pine needle stuck in me," she replied. "Will you get it out?"

As the man looked, he saw the pine needle had embedded itself in the girl's very private spot.

"Oh no," he replied, "I can't. This is Forestry Commission land and it says over there on that notice board that no timber must be moved from recreational areas."

★ ★ ★

"It's not fair," moaned the young woman to her elderly aunt. "We've been married for three years and I still can't get pregnant. Yet all you ever hear about is girls who sleep with men once and get caught."

"Very true," replied her aunt thoughtfully, "but that only happens if you're single."

★ ★ ★

A man was getting married and was concerned that his wife might not be a virgin, although she'd said she was one.

"I tell you what to do," said his mate. "Go out and buy three pots of paint – yellow, blue and green. Also buy a hammer."

"But I don't understand," protested the man. "What's that going to prove?"

"Patience, patience," said his mate, "and I'll tell you. Paint your todger in yellow, blue and green stripes, then show it to your girlfriend. If she reacts by saying "I've never seen one with stripes before, then you hit her over the head with your hammer."

"How did it go last night, lover boy?" asked his mate.

"Fine, I think. Mind, she's a bit odd. She likes it in her ear."

"Really?"

"Yeah. Cos every time I tried to put it in her mouth, she kept turning her head."

★ ★ ★

For three months, the young ambitious executive had been secretly having an affair with the dynamic managing director of an international company. Whenever it was possible, they would go to his flat in the city and spend some hours tumbling among the sheets. One day, as he walked out of the shower back into the bedroom, she looked at him and asked

"Why is it that you're going grey on top but down below it's still a deep rich brown?"

"Quite simple, my dear," he replied arrogantly. "I've never had any worries down below."

★ ★ ★

"It's no good," said his new girlfriend.

"I can't feel a thing, I'm afraid your organ is too small."

"Is that so?" he retorted, "perhaps that's because I didn't realise I'd be playing in a cathedral."

★ ★ ★

The newly married wife was not happy with her husband's lovemaking technique. The trouble was that he was too rough – in, thrash about, all over. She decided to try and teach him gentler ways. When they went to bed that night, she persuaded him to try a different method.

"I'm going to put 10 pence on each shoulder, 50 pence on your back and 5 pence on your bum. As you say each coin, I want you to move the corresponding part of your body."

"Okay," he agreed. "10 pence, 10 pence, 50 pence, 5 pence." As he said these words, he moved accordingly and the lovemaking was much more gentle.

"10 pence, 10 pence, 50 pence, 5 pence," he said, repeating it over and over again.

"Oooh, that's wonderful," whispered his wife joyously.

"10 pence, 10 pence, 50 pence, 5 pence," he gasped.

"Oh yes, oh yes," she cried.

"10 pence, 10 pence, 50 pence, 5 pence," he panted.

"Again, again," she cried.

"10 pence, 10 pence, 50 pence... oh bugger it," he cried, "75p, 75p, 75p ...."

★ ★ ★

The young girl and her father were at loggerheads about who she should marry. The father wanted her to wed Lionel – short, fat but very rich. She wanted Troy – tall, dark and handsome. Eventually, the father decided that the two men would have to compete against each other in a race and whoever won would marry his daughter.

First the men would have to run 1500 metres, then complete a gruelling obstacle course and finally swim across the river. The great day dawned and as 8 o'clock chimed, the two men set off. By the time they had completed the first two stages, Troy had a comfortable lead, but the daughter was anxious. To spur him on, she stripped off and standing on the other side of the river, she beckoned to him provocatively. At first, he lengthened his stroke but suddenly he began floundering and to her horror, Lionel caught up, passed him and eventually won the race. Later, as Lionel and the daughter prepared for marriage, she saw the defeated Troy and said angrily

"You silly prat, what happened? You were winning easily."

"I know," he replied sadly. "It was all going well until you took your clothes off and then I started picking up weed!"

★ ★ ★

"Ooh your kisses really burn," she said.
"Woops, sorry, I'll put my cigarette out," he replied.

★ ★ ★

Three young bucks were boasting about their sexual experiences.
"Older women, that's what you want," said a skinny youth of 19.
"Last week I shagged the barmaid from the Black Pig. What a mover! She must be pushing 35."
"That's nothing," said the second youth, scornfully. "I picked up a bird on holiday and she was in her forties. She could show you a thing or two," he laughed.
They both looked at the other lad who was sitting there staring into space.
"Come on Steve, what about you?" they asked.
"I had it off with a woman of 23," he said dreamily.
"Too young, too young," they jeered. "Hey but I was only 12 at the time," he continued.

★ ★ ★

Sitting with his arms around her on the sofa, Gerald whispered in her ear
"Come on 'chelle, it's only a week to go before the wedding, how about giving me a hint of what's to come."
She shook her head adamantly.
"No Gerald, we promised we'd wait until we were married."

"Oh go on," he persisted. "Just a quick feel of your tits."

So she relented and gave him a quick feel. He could hardly contain himself.

"Oh 'chelle, 'chelle, you drive me wild. I can hardly wait. Please let me just have a quick sniff of your pussy." Now Michelle was also feeling aroused but she was determined not to spoil their big day.

"Okay, but no touching," she said.

She dropped her knickers and let him have a quick sniff.

"Gosh 'chelle!" he exclaimed, "are you sure it's going to last another week?"

★　★　★

Every day for six months, Colin had passed the local Chinese take-away time and time again, just to get a glimpse of the beautiful girl behind the counter. He couldn't eat, he couldn't sleep. All he could think about was his little eastern delight. One day, he had a couple of neat whiskies and plucked up the courage to go in and invite her out to the cinema. And she agreed! He was ecstatic. The following week, they went to see a romance at the local flicks, they walked back under the moonlight and he invited her in for coffee. Later, he put his arm around her, nibbled her ear and tentatively put his hand on her breasts. She didn't push him away so he was encouraged to go further. Soon, they were shagging away in bed, not once but three times. Eventually she started to fall asleep but Colin was still full of lust. He leant over and whispered in her ear

"How about a 69 before we go to sleep?"

To his amazement, she sat up angrily and replied

"Listen, you selfish prat. I've put up with you pawing me all night. I've let you screw me three times, and I have to say you're not very good, there's no bloody way I'm going to start cooking at this time of the morning!"

★ ★ ★

Karl was God's gift to women, or so he thought. Clubbing it every night, he would pick up a different girl three or four times a week and in no time at all smooth-talk them into bed. On Friday night, he arrived home with his latest catch, a young girl called Sandra. Soon, they were in the bedroom and as he began stripping off to reveal his perfect body, Sandra noticed two tattoos. One on his right shoulder, the other on his lower back.

"What's that then?" she said, pointing to his shoulder.

"Oh that's a lily," he replied. "I used to go out with a girl called Lily. She was all right, so I got this to remind me of her."

"So what's that?" she said, pointing to his back.

"That's a tiger. It reminds me of another girl who loved me. Her nick name was Tiger because she was really feisty. Cor what a girl!"

By this time Sandra was a bit fed up with talking about his ex's, but she gasped in astonishment when he dropped his pants to reveal a strange symbol on his todger.

"Don't tell me that's another of your girlfriends?" she sneered.

"Oh no, luv," he said smiling, "that's a BT symbol."

"What d'you mean?"
Karl lunged towards her and said
"It's for yoo-hoo."

★ ★ ★

The couple had been courting for almost a year when they decided to get married. James was over the moon. He had always wanted to marry a true blonde and although they had saved themselves for the big day, she assured him she was blonde, through and through. Some months after the wedding, James happened to notice one day that his wife's pubes were turning black.

"Hey!" he cried. "You told me you were a true blonde."

"But I am," she lied, thinking quickly. "It's like this James. You know when you hit your nail with a hammer, it goes all black?"

"Yeah," he replied suspiciously.

"Well, come on James, you can't deny you've been giving this some hammer these last few months."

★ ★ ★

It was Fiona's birthday and her rich boyfriend gave her a beautiful fur coat made out of skunk.

"Good gracious!" she exclaimed, "it's hard to believe that such a fabulous coat could come from such a stinking little beast."

"Okay, that's enough, give me it back," replied the boyfriend angrily. "I wasn't looking for thanks, but I object to you being so personal."

★ ★ ★

"Coming back to my place for coffee?" asked the man on their first date.

"Yeah, sure," she replied.

Later, sitting on the sofa, she remarked

"You don't talk much."

"Don't need to darling," he said, pulling down his trousers, "this does all the talking for me."

"Well, that doesn't say much either," she retorted.

★ ★ ★

It was love at first sight. The young couple met in the Spring and were married the following October. During their courting, they had played around but one thing she would never do was give him oral sex.

"No, I'll never do that, all your respect for me will go," she would say.

And because he loved her so much, he didn't make a big fuss. The years went by, now and again, he would bring up the subject but she would always refuse.

"You'll have no respect for me," she would say.

Then the day dawned on their ruby wedding anniversary and he turned to her in bed and said

"Oh Cheryl, we've had a good life, and a successful one. Look at this lovely house, two kids at University and a 'round-the-world cruise booked for next month. How could I not respect you? Let's have some oral sex. Just this once." So, after all

those years, she gave in. Later, as they were relaxing, there was a ring at the doorbell. He turned to her and said "You go answer that, cocksucker."

★ ★ ★

The latest au pair was a beautiful blonde 18-year-old from Sweden. As soon as the eldest son of the house saw her, he fell instantly in love and was determined to make himself known to her. However, it was a few months later before anything happened because he spent the summer overseas at a soccer school in Germany. Within the first week of his return, they became firm friends and on the Sunday night, they went to bed. Oh the shame! He couldn't get Percy to perform, maybe he was trying too hard.

Blushing with embarrassment, he stuttered his apology to the au pair.

"Oh don't worry," she said. "Sometimes your father has trouble too."

★ ★ ★

From a very early age, the little boy had been interested in politics. He would listen to all the debates and gaze lovingly at the White House. As time went on, the interest didn't waiver and by the time he got to University, he was making a name for himself as a good speaker on local issues. By the time he was middle-aged, he ran for the Presidency and was successful. When he thanked the country for their support, he also mentioned mysteriously "and a special thought goes to Mr Wilkins, good luck tonight sir." No matter how hard the journalists tried, he would never explain that last remark, and so it remained a mystery. However, many years later in his old age he was being interviewed on television because his biography had just been published. One eager journalist had studied the man's life very carefully and he rediscovered the strange remark.

"Okay," said the man. "I guess it will be all right to tell you now. When I was a little boy, I used to play in the garden till quite late at night. One hot evening, the bedroom window of the next door neighbours was open and I couldn't help but hear Mrs Wilkins say

"Oral sex! You must be joking. Let me tell you Albert Wilkins that you'll get oral sex when the boy next door becomes President!"

★ ★ ★

"Hello Fiona, I hear you had a date with Clive last night. Was he nice?"

"I've only got one thing to say," she replied, "my legs are my best friends."

"Oh. So no good, huh?"

When Christmas came, the two girls met at a disco. Fiona was smiling happily.

"You look as if life's good," remarked her friend.

"So how did the date go, Fiona?" asked her friend.

"My legs are my best friends," she replied mysteriously.

"What does that mean?"

"It means he was a prat so I walked home."

Sometime later, the two girls met up again.

"Oh yes," replied Fiona, "I've met this gorgeous guy and let's just say, even the best of friends must part."

★ ★ ★

There are three stages of sex in a couple's married life.

Stage one is anytime, anywhere, when you're first married, the urge can happen at any time.

Stage two is when you've been married for some time and the sex is usually confined to the bedroom.

Stage three happens after many years of marriage. It's when couples pass each other in the hall and say "Fuck you."

★ ★ ★

The man had had a bad day at work and now his girlfriend was late meeting him in the pub. Eventually she arrived looking flustered.

"Oh Geoffrey," she said, "I've got some good news and some bad news."

"Cut the crap," he replied angrily. "I'm in no mood for games. Just tell me the good news."

"Okay," she said. "The good news is that you're not firing blanks."

★ ★ ★

An arrogant bodybuilder picked up a girl at a dance and took her back to his place. As he stripped off his shirt and flexed his muscles, he remarked "Take a look at this, darling, 500lbs of pure dynamite."

She was suitably impressed.

Then he dropped his trousers and showed off his bulging thigh muscles.

"And there's another 500lbs of dynamite," he boasted.

What a hulk, thought the girl, this is going to be quite a night and she waited with growing anticipation. The bodybuilder then dropped his shorts and the girl gasped loudly and walked towards the door.

"Hey darling, what's wrong," he said puzzled.

"Listen Mr Muscles," she replied scornfully. "With all that dynamite and such a short fuse, I'm taking cover before you blow."

★ ★ ★

"Go on, Julie," coaxed the man. "If I get this car up to 100, will you take your clothes off?"

She finally agrees and when he hits 100, she starts to strip. Unfortunately his eyes linger on her just a little too long and the car careers off the road and crashes into a ditch. The girl is thrown clear but the man is trapped.

"Go and get help," he gasps.

"I can't," she says. "I haven't got any clothes on."

"Just go," he urges. "Look, my shoe's lying over there, use it to cover yourself and hurry."

Just round the corner she spots a garage and runs up to it in great distress.

"Oh please help me," she cries, on seeing the mechanic. "My boyfriend's stuck."

The man looks down at the shoe covering her crotch and replies "I'm sorry love, there's not a lot I can do, he's too far in."

★ ★ ★

John sat down and put pen to paper.

"My dear Lucy, can you ever forgive me? I'd had a lot of pressure at work and I wasn't thinking straight when I broke off our engagement. Of course I love you more than anything in the world. Let's not let my moment of madness spoil our future happiness.

Hugs & kisses

John

P.S. Congratulations on winning top prize on the lottery."

★ ★ ★

Tracy was worried. Her boyfriend seemed to be cooling and she couldn't bear the thought he might leave her for another woman. She decided to give him a surprise and had a great idea of having his initials tattooed on her backside. His name was Brian Bates so she had B tattooed on either cheek.

That night, on going to bed, Tracy stripped off, bent over and said "What do you think of this then?"

Brian retorted angrily "You bloody tart, who the hell's Bob."

★ ★ ★

"Doctor, doctor, I think there's something terribly wrong with me," said the agitated man. He went on to describe his symptoms.

"The first time I made love, I felt warm and restful and comfortable all over. But the second time I couldn't stop shivering, I was so cold and covered in goose pimples."

"Mmm," replied the doctor, "that sounds very unusual, I'd better give you a thorough examination."

But nothing seemed amiss so the doctor sent for the man's wife and told her about the odd complaint.

"He felt warm and comfortable the first time, but cold and shivery the second."

The wife snorted with contempt. "I'm not surprised," she said. "The first time was in summer and the second time was in mid-December!"

★ ★ ★

A young man had been going out with his girlfriend for two months and decided he would like to buy her a present, but something that was not too personal in case she thought he was getting too serious. Unsure of what to buy, he asked his sister to go with him to the shops and after looking around, he decided to buy some gloves. As the young man made the purchase, his sister also did some shopping and bought a pair of knickers. Unfortunately, in wrapping up the two purchases, the attendant got them muddled up so the young man got the knickers. He never thought to check, he simply wrote a letter to go with the gift and posted the parcel that evening. His letter read:

"My darling Debs,

Hope you like this little gift. I bought them because I noticed you didn't wear any when we go out in the evenings. My sister would have chosen the long ones but I think the shorter ones are easier to get off. I hope the colour's to your liking. The shop assistant had a pair the same colour and she showed me the ones she'd been wearing for the past two months and they were hardly soiled. She was very helpful. She tried yours on for me so that I could see what they looked like. I wish I could be there when you first put them on, but as I'm not meeting you until Saturday I suppose others will see them before I do.

Until then, all my love

Dave.

P.S. The shop assistant also gave me a little tip. When you take them off, blow in them before putting them away as they will be a little damp from wearing, of course."

* * *

A young, naive girl had been asked out by the local romeo and before she went, her grandmother gave her a few words of warning.

"Remember my dear," she said, "he will try to kiss you and run his hands over your breasts. It will feel nice, but you mustn't let him do it."

She continued "And then he will try and put his hands between your legs, but again you must resist him. And then

my dear," she said most solemnly, "he will try to get on top of you and have his way with you. Don't ever let him do that, it will disgrace the family."

The following day, the girl went round to see her grandmother and tell her what had happened.

"Oh grandma, you were right," she said. "He did try to get on top of me, but I didn't disgrace the family." She continued triumphantly, "When he tried, I turned him over, got on top and disgraced his family!"

★　★　★

After their first date, the young man drove his girlfriend home and as he turned into her street he put his hand on her knee.

"I've only got three words to say to you," she said. "You dirty bugger."

Nothing more was said until he pulled up outside her door, and then he remarked

"And I have only three words to say to you 'please let go.'"

★　★　★

Maurice picked a girl up at a disco, and after a couple of dances he whispered in her ear, "Hey luv, how about a fuck?"

Astonished at his crude language, the girl pretended not to hear and went on dancing.

Maurice leaned over and asked her a second time, but again she didn't answer.

However, he persisted and after a third time, she replied forcibly "Is this what you say to every girl you go out with?"

"Oh yes," he replied.

"Well, you must lose a lot of girls with that attitude," she retorted.

"Oh I do," he said, "but I also get a lot of fucks."

★ ★ ★

Two middle-aged bachelors had shared a house for many years and it was with great sadness that one day they realised they had hit hard times.

"It's no good, Jack," said Marvin. "We'll have to get rid of our last remaining chicken, we'll eat her for lunch tomorrow."

The following day dawned and it was Jack's turn to cook, so he prepared the bird and put it in the oven. However some hours later Marvin arrived home to find the kitchen full of smoke, the bird blackened and charred, and Jack nowhere to be found.

Marvin searched the house and eventually found Jack in the garden shed, with his head between the legs of their faithful old cleaner, Janet.

"Damn you Jack," snarled Marvin, "you really are a first-class prat. First you fuck the only bird we've got to eat, and secondly you eat the only bird we've got to fuck."

★ ★ ★

As a 'thank you' to his father's estate workers, the eldest son would dress up as Father Christmas each year and visit every house with a sackful of toys. This year, he arrived at the third house and tiptoed into the bedroom, only to be confronted by

a beautiful young woman who sat up in bed when she heard his footsteps.

"Oh, I'm so sorry," said Father Christmas. "I thought this was Bobby's room."

"No, he's next door," she whispered. "But don't go, stay awhile," and with that she dropped the sheet to reveal a see-through nightie.

"No, no," said Father Christmas blushing, "I've got a busy night ahead of me."

"Oh, come on," she urged, slowly disrobing. "A few more minutes won't make that much difference."

"I'm sorry I can't," he replied, now feeling very hot under the collar.

"Oh please," she said, jumping naked out of bed.

"Oh bugger it!" he exclaimed, putting down the sack of toys. "I wouldn't get back up the chimney like this anyway."

★ ★ ★

It was their first date and Jack was completely infatuated by his beautiful partner. He couldn't wait to get her into bed so it wasn't long before they were in the throes of passion. One thing that struck Jack as strange was that every time he thrust forward, the girl's toes would curl up. Later, when they had finished and showered, they felt their passion rising and were soon back in bed for a second time. It was just as good as before, but Jack noticed that now her toes did not curl. When sometime had passed, he asked her curiously "Why is that the first time in bed your toes curled up, and the second time, they didn't?"

She laughed and replied "The second time I'd had a shower and taken my tights off."

★ ★ ★

A horny man picks up a girl at a nightclub and takes her back to his flat, where he soon persuades her into bed. Crash, bang, wallop – it's all over in a flash. The man turns to the girl and says, "If I'd known you were a virgin, I'd have gone slower."
"No kidding," she replies "If I thought you could've controlled yourself a little longer, I'd have taken my knickers off."

★ ★ ★

A man leant over the counter and said to the barmaid "I don't 'arf fancy you, luv. How about a quickie when the pub closes."
She looked at him and said "Listen fella, I've been on my feet all day. I'm tired."
"Well that's okay, we'll lie down instead," he replied.

★ ★ ★

Karl met a woman in a pub and asked her if she would like a drink.
"No thanks," she replied. "I don't drink alcohol."
"How about a cigarette?"
She shook her head. "I don't smoke," she replied.
"Packet of crisps?"

Again she shook her head. Secretly congratulating himself on spending so little, he asked her if he could see her home and when she said 'yes,' he was delighted.

They arrived at her front door, and in the hall was a dead horse. Seeing the look on his face, she said "Well I didn't say I was tidy."

★ ★ ★

He picked her up at a nightclub, and they woke up the next morning in her bed. Suddenly the phone rang and he answered it. "Just a moment," he said, putting his hand over the mouthpiece. "It's for a Miss Julie Quick. Is that you?"

★ ★ ★

MEET THE MEDICS

"Doctor, doctor, every bone in my body hurts."
"Then be thankful you're not a kipper."

★ ★ ★

"Well Mr Bates, I'm very pleased with your progress. Your new hand transplant has gone well and I think you're well on the way to a full recovery. Any problems?" asked the surgeon.
"As a matter of fact, there is," replied the man. "You gave me a female hand and every time I go for a pee, it won't let go."

★ ★ ★

"Doctor, doctor, I'm so knackered!" cried the distraught man. "I just can't get to sleep at night."
"Now calm down," said the doctor. "You're obviously suffering from nerves, you must learn to relax. When you go to bed tonight, start with your toes and gently relax all your body, bit by bit."
So that night, the man got into bed and said to himself
"Right toes, go to sleep. Now feet, go to sleep. Now ankles go to sleep. Now knees go to..."

But before he could continue, his wife walked seductively into the bedroom, wearing the skimpiest baby doll nightie.

"Okay, wake up everyone," he called.

★ ★ ★

"Every time I look in the mirror, I see an old man, tired and haggard."

"Well at least your eyesight's perfect," replied the doctor.

★ ★ ★

Did you hear about the plastic surgeon who was sued by one of his female patients?

She'd had so many facelifts, she now had a beard.

★ ★ ★

A woman read in a book an old remedy for curing piles. Now she suffered badly, so she decided to try it out and following instructions, she stuck some tea leaves up her backside. Alas, the remedy didn't work, so she was forced to go to the doctors.

"Bend over please," he said examining her. "Well I can't see much but I can forecast that you'll soon meet a tall dark handsome man and have three children."

★ ★ ★

The woman went along to the optician's for an eye test.

"Right, Mrs Grimshaw, we'll start with the bottom line. Can you read the letters for me?"

She squinted at them for a moment and replied "No I can't."

"Well, not to worry, let's try the next line up."

But she couldn't read it. In fact, she couldn't read any of them, not even the largest letter at the top.

"Oh dear, can you see this?" said the optician impatiently, as he unzipped his trousers and showed her his willy.

"Oh yes, I can see that," she replied.

"Ah, ha!" he exclaimed. "Of course. I should have known what was wrong, you're cock-eyed."

★ ★ ★

A woman is so upset about her flat chest, she tells her husband she wants to go to a plastic surgeon.

"Hold on a minute," replies the man, "before you go, try rubbing toilet paper on your nipples for the next few days."

"But why? I don't understand. Will it make them bigger?"

"Bound to. Look what it did for your arse."

★ ★ ★

The worried man went to the doctors.

"I think I'm impotent," he said. "I can't make love to my wife."

"I see," said the doctor. "I suggest both you and your wife come and see me next week and I'll see what we can do. They turned up the following Tuesday and while the husband stayed in the outer room, the doctor took the wife into the cubicle. He asked her to undress and then walk up and down for him. This she did, while he inspected her thoroughly.

"Okay, you can get dressed now," he finally said, "while I go and have a quick word with your husband."

The doctor went back into the outer room and shook his head sadly.

"What a shame. As a matter of fact, there's nothing wrong with you," he said. "Your wife doesn't give me an erection either."

★　★　★

"I'm sorry, my glasses have broken again," said the man to the optician.

"Oh dear," replied the optician. "It's becoming a bit of a habit. What happened this time?"

"Well, I was kissing my girlfriend when it happened."

"Really?! I can't see why that should break your glasses."

"She crossed her legs," he replied.

★　★　★

There are only two men in the waiting room. One has a bandage around his head, the other is covered in food. There are bits of spaghetti in his hair, egg on his tie, jelly on his trousers and his face is splattered with gravy. This man speaks

"I see your head is bandaged up, is it serious?"

"Oh no, not too bad," replies the other.

"I happened to walk into a lamp post and suffered some concussion. How about you?"

"Oh, I'm just not eating properly," he answers.

★ ★ ★

Bob was a bit taken aback when he walked into the surgery to be greeted by a beautiful, young doctor. She smiled at him and he felt himself get hot under the collar.

"All right Mr Taylor, please go behind the screen and strip off."

As he sat there, naked, she put her gentle hands on his body and said "say 99 please."

By this time, Bob was back in full control. He smiled and began "1... 2... 3."

★ ★ ★

"I'm very disappointed," said the doctor to his patient. "If you're committed to curing this nervous problem, you must come and see me on a regular basis. Yet it's nearly a month since you missed your last appointment."

The man replied sullenly

"I was only doing what you said."

"What's that supposed to mean. What did I say?"

"You told me to keep away from anyone who got on my nerves."

★ ★ ★

The woman rushed into the chemist's, crying.

"Do you realise what you've done?" she wailed. "You gave my husband rat poison instead of stomach salts."

"Oh dear," replied the chemist. "That is awful, you owe me another £2."

★ ★ ★

There were only two people in the doctor's waiting room. Robert had come for a blood test and was sitting opposite a man who was constantly mumbling to himself.

"Please let me be ill, please, please let me be ill."

Unable to contain his curiosity any longer, Robert asked the man "I'm sorry, I couldn't help but overhear you say you hoped you were sick. Why is that?"

The man replied sadly

"I hate to be well and feel like this!"

★ ★ ★

"And what about your love life?" the psychiatrist asked the woman.

"Well, it's like Bonfire Night," she replied.

"I see. You mean it's full of fun, coloured lights and lots of big bangs?"

"No," she said scornfully. "It's once a year."

★ ★ ★

The man rushed into the chemist's and asked
"Have you got anything to stop a terrible bout of hiccups?"
Without warning, the chemist immediately slapped him hard across the face.
"There," he said triumphantly. "I bet that's stopped them.
The man stood there stunned, his cheek turning bright red and replied
"It's for my wife waiting outside in the car."

★ ★ ★

"Doctor, doctor," shouted the distressed receptionist, "that man you pronounced fit and well a few minutes ago has dropped down dead outside the surgery."
The doctor replied calmly
"Don't worry Beth, turn him round so he looks as if he's just coming in."

★ ★ ★

The great consultant looked down his nose at the scruffy man who shuffled into the room. After a quick examination, he asked
"Have you been to see anyone else before coming to see me?"
"Yes, Dr Peek," he replied warily.
"Dr Peek! That charlatan!" exclaimed the consultant, "and I suppose he fed you lots of useless pills and doled out some pathetic advice?"
"I don't know, he told me to come and see you."

★ ★ ★

The man came round from the operation to remove his appendix but was puzzled to see there was also a bandage round his private parts. On the next ward round, he asked his consultant why this was so.

"Ah, you see," said the consultant calmly, "we had a small accident. I did such a beautiful job sewing up your appendix cut that everyone clapped and cheered. So I took a bow, forgetting I still had a knife in my hand, and accidentally cut your willy off."

★ ★ ★

The professor was lecturing his students on plastic surgery. At one point he asked them what they would do if someone was born without a penis. A hand shot up at the back and a boy answered

"Wait until she'd grown up and then give her one."

★ ★ ★

"What's up Jack?" asked his mate.

"It's the wife. She introduced me to her psychiatrist this morning. She said 'This is Jack, my husband, one of the men I was telling you about.'"

★ ★ ★

"Doctor, doctor," cried the man in despair. "I've got such terrible bad breath. It's having a dreadful effect on my love life. I can't get a girl to come near me. What shall I do?"

The doctor thought for a moment and replied

"You have two chances. You either stop scratching your bum, or you stop biting your nails."

★ ★ ★

The Lord Mayor and Mayoress were touring the new wing of a hospital. As they passed through the male ward, the Mayoress spotted a man frantically masturbating.

"What on earth's gong on over there?" she asked.

The doctor explained that the poor man had something wrong with his reproductive organs and if he didn't relieve himself twice a day, then the pain was unbearable.

A few minutes later, they passed some side rooms, off the main ward. Through the window of the third room, they saw a nurse giving the patient oral sex.

"And what's the meaning of this?" asked the Mayor.

"Same problem as the other man," replied the doctor, "but this one has private medical insurance."

★ ★ ★

A twenty-stone man was desperate to lose weight and as he scanned the personal column of the local newspaper, he read an advertisement, guaranteeing instant weight loss. He rang the number and was told that someone from the company would be round the next morning.

"How much weight do you want to lose?" he was asked.

"Well, I thought I would start with half a stone."

So the next morning, the bell rang and there on the doorstep was a beautiful brunette. She came in, stripped off to her undies and told him he could have her, if he caught her.

For thirty minutes, he chased her round the house, upstairs and downstairs, time and time again. Then after thirty minutes, she gave in and they had sex on the dining room floor.

"Now go and weigh yourself," she said, and indeed, he had lost half a stone. He gave her £200 and she left.

A couple of days went by and the man rang the company again, telling them that this time he wanted to lose a stone. The next morning he opened the door to find a stunning blonde. As she dropped her coat, he saw she had nothing on underneath.

"If you catch me, you can have me," she cooed and for a whole hour he chased her round the house and the garden until they fell exhausted into bed. Later, he weighed himself and found he was a stone lighter. He paid £400 and she left.

So a week went by, but the man couldn't get those amazing experiences out of his mind. He rang the company for a third time and told them he wanted to lose two stone.

"Are you absolutely sure you want to lose so much in one go?" he was asked.

"Yes, yes," he replied impatiently. The next morning there was a loud knocking on the door.

"Come in, come in," he called.

To his horror, the room darkened as a huge gorilla-type man walked into the room.

"Right," he bellowed. "Get going. This time I chase you, and when I catch you, you're fucked."

★ ★ ★

An estate agent suffers a serious accident and is rushed unconscious to hospital. When he wakes up he finds the curtains drawn round him and asks the nurse for an explanation.

"Not to worry," she says, "it's simply a precaution. A building across the street has gone up in flames and we didn't want you waking up, thinking you'd died."

★ ★ ★

One of the benefactors of the local lunatic asylum is walking around the wards when he sees a man sitting bolt upright in bed pretending to drive and making car noises.

"How are you?" asks the visitor.

"Knackered," replies the patient. "I've had to drive all the way to Scotland to deliver a load of steel."

In the next bed, the patient is frantically moving up and down underneath the covers.

"Everything all right?" he asks, pulling back the bedclothes to reveal a naked man lying face downwards.

"You bet," grins the man. "I'm shagging his wife while he's in Scotland."

★ ★ ★

"Okay John," said the psychiatrist. "I'm going to drop some paint on this piece of paper and I want you to tell me what you see."

"That looks like Naomi Campbell with no clothes on," said John, looking at the first blob.

"And that looks like my next-door neighbour, Connie, taking a bath," he replied, pointing to the second.

"And that one looks like your receptionist, lying naked on the ground."

"Mmm," replied the psychiatrist, "it's obvious you're obsessed with sex."

"Now just hold on a minute!" John retorted. "You're the one drawing the dirty pictures."

★ ★ ★

"Oh doctor," said the distraught patient. "Why do so many people take an instant dislike to me?"

"Saves time," came the reply.

★ ★ ★

The woman went for her weekly appointment with the psychiatrist.

"So Mrs Freelot, what have your dreams been about this week?"

"I haven't had any," she replied.

"Oh dear," he said sighing deeply. "How can I help you, if you won't do your homework?"

★ ★ ★

An arrogant man went to the doctor's and after a complete examination was told he either had V.D. or mumps. The doctor told him to come back the following day for his test results when he told him

"I'm sorry Mr Squires, I'm afraid you have V.D."

"Well I knew that," said the man scornfully. "How on earth would I come in contact with the mumps."

★ ★ ★

A woman goes to the doctor's because she's at her wits end. For months she's tried to get a boyfriend but no one is interested, and her need to have a loving relationship is making her desperate. Having spent a fortune on good clothes and evocative perfume to no avail, she tells the doctor of her plight.

The doctor soon realises that she needs to see a sex therapist so he refers her to Doctor Choy Nang.

"Harro," says the doctor, "what can I do for you, prease."

The woman relates her sad story and the doctor tells her he will have to run a series of tests.

"Preese take off your clothes," he says.

She does this and stands in front of him while he looks at her very carefully.

"Now preese, on hands and knees and crawl around the room." Although astonished at his request, she does as he wishes.

"Ah ha," he says, smiling broadly. "I know what problem is, you have Ed Zachany disease."

The woman gasps, "Oh no, what's that?"

"It mean your face look Ed Zachany like your arse."

★ ★ ★

The man lay down on the psychiatrist's couch and unburdened his problems.

"It all started when I was a teenager. At 15, I really wanted a girlfriend. Then when I found one at 17, she was so dull, I couldn't bear it. I needed a bit of passion in my life, so I dated this girl at work but she was so emotional – crying with happiness, crying with sadness – that it wore me out. I dumped her and went out with someone a little less demonstrative. But she was boring. I decided I needed excitement in my life, so I found a girl who was a real party animal. We'd be out every night, never getting back till dawn and I was really knackered. Half the time I didn't know where she was or who she was with! It was all too much, so I decided to look for someone much more focused, someone who was going places. I found her all right. We got married, but she wanted better things, so she divorced me and took everything I owned. So, doc, all I want now is a girl with big tits."

★　★　★

A young couple were about to get married. The husband-to-be was ecstatic that such a gorgeous creature would want to marry such a boring old fart as himself. First they had to get the all clear from the doctor's. A few days after the examinations, the doctor asked the young man to come in for the results.

"Ah Mr Brownall, do come in. I have some good news and some bad news."

"Oh no," replied the poor man. "What's the bad news?"

"Your wife-to-be has herpes."

"Bloody hell!" he exclaimed. "What's the good news?"

"She didn't get it from you."

★　★　★

"Come in Mr Burton," said the doctor solemnly.

"I've had the results of your tests and I've got some good news and some bad news."

"What's the bad news?" asked the man anxiously.

"I'm afraid you have a rare illness picked up from your expeditions into the jungle. There's no cure. In fact, within the next 24 hours, you'll go into a coma and die."

The man gasped in pain. "Then what the hell's the good news?" he asked.

The doctor's face lit up with anticipation.

"I've just taken on a new receptionist, the one with the big tits, and she's agreed to go out with me tonight."

* * *

A man went for his annual examination at the hospital and as he removed his trousers he revealed his penis was the size of a little "pinkie." Unfortunately, the nurses weren't quick enough to hide their amusement and the man retorted angrily,
"Hey, it's the uniforms, I can't help getting a hard-on when I see them."

* * *

A man was referred to a psychiatrist who decided to start off by testing him with word association.
"I'm going to repeat the same word over and over again and I want you to tell me what comes into your mind. Are you ready? Good. The word is breasts."
"Melons," replied the man.
"Breasts."
"Grapefruit," said the man.
"Breasts."
"Oranges."
"Breasts."
"Windscreen wipers."
"Hold on a minute. Windscreen wipers? I don't understand."
"It's easy," smiled the man. "First, this one, then that one, then this one...."

* * *

"Doctor, doctor," cried the man in anguish. "When I woke up this morning I thought I was a horse. Now all I can eat is oats and graze on the grass in my garden."

"Really!" replied the doctor. "Now that's very interesting. Would you mind coming to graze round at my house, the roses could do with some good horse shit."

★ ★ ★

Late in the afternoon, the phone rang and Bob answered it.

"Hello Mr Naylor, I'm afraid I have some bad news and some really bad news for you," said the doctor.

"Oh hell!" exclaimed Bob "What is it?"

"I'm sorry to tell you that you only have 12 hours to live."

"What!" he gasped. "Well, what can be worse than that?"

"I meant to call you first thing this morning."

★ ★ ★

A bloke went to a specialist because his todger had turned bright red.

"Mmm, we'll soon put that right," said the doctor, and after messing around with it for a few minutes, it was back to normal.

"That's great," said the man. "How much do I owe you?"

"Just £20."

The following Sunday he was telling his mate about it in the pub.

"Well, to be honest," confessed his mate, "I think I've got something similar, only mine is a yellowy green colour. He sounds good, and cheap, I think I'll go and see him."

"Mmm," said the specialist thoughtfully. "Well I can do something for you, but it's quite a complicated treatment and will cost you £3,000."

"What!" exclaimed the man. "You only charged my mate £20."

"Yes, indeed," replied the specialist, "but he just had lipstick on his. You've got gangrene."

★ ★ ★

An old woman goes to the doctor's to get the results of her tests.

"Sit down, Mrs Chivers," says the doctor kindly, "I'm afraid the news isn't very good."

"Tell me the worst," she replies.

"Well, there are two things. First you have cancer..."

"Oh no," she gasps.

"...And secondly, you have Alzheimer's disease."

"Oh thank goodness for that," she says smiling, "for a moment I thought you were going to tell me I had cancer."

★ ★ ★

"Mrs Lotsovit," asks the doctor, "do you smoke after sexual intercourse?"

"Ooh, I don't know," she replied. "I've never bothered to look."

★ ★ ★

A man went to the doctor's because he was having trouble with his sex life. He hoped the doctor would be able to cure him of premature ejaculation. The doctor advised him that when he was getting to the point of no return, he should give himself a shock and that would help prolong his lovemaking. Eager to try it out as soon as possible, the man bought a starting pistol and rushed home immediately. To his delight his wife was in bed, naked, waiting for him. Without a second thought, he jumped into bed and they were soon having oral sex. Then as he felt ejaculation coming on, he reached for the gun and fired it. The following day, the man went back to the doctor. He was asked whether it was a success.

"Well, not really," he replied. "When I fired the gun, my wife had a heart attack and bit the top of my penis off, while our next-door neighbour came out of the wardrobe with his hands in the air."

★ ★ ★

MEET THE NEIGHBOURS

"Do you know, Ethel, it's quite true that if you talk to your plants they will flourish. It's like our Jack telling me, if he treats his cow with affection, she'll give more milk."

"Now that I understand," replied her neighbour, "so will the milkman."

★ ★ ★

Every day Bob would watch his neighbour, Al, mount his bicycle and set off for the station, while his wife would run along behind, sweating and panting. Eventually, curiosity got the better of him and the next time he saw Al in the pub, he asked

"Why is it you bicycle to the station every morning while your wife runs along behind you?"

"Oh that's easy," replied Al, "she hasn't got a bicycle."

★ ★ ★

"Our next door neighbours are going to collect a great deal of insurance money from the coach accident."

"But wait a minute, they weren't in the coach."

"That's true, but the wife was quick thinking and broke both her husband's legs."

★ ★ ★

Two neighbours talking over the garden wall.
"Poor old Jackie from number 6. I hear she's got that eating disorder... you know, bulimia. That's why she's so thin."
"Oh no," replied the other. "It's not bulimia that makes her so thin. It's her husband. Every time he strips off, she throws up."

★ ★ ★

Thirty five years ago, Molly was digging in the back garden when she lost her beautiful emerald engagement ring. Yesterday, her son was planting potatoes in exactly the same place when he suffered a heart attack. What an amazing coincidence!

★ ★ ★

Two neighbours had been at each other's throats for years over a disputed boundary wall.
"I bet you didn't know that most people round here call you 'piles'," said the first man angrily, "and that's because you're such a bloody pain in the arse."
"Oh really," retorted the second man, "and you're known locally as 'virgin'."
"Bugger off, I've had more women than you've had hot dinners. Why call me virgin?"
"Because you're an ignorant twat."

★ ★ ★

"Hey Beryl!" shouted Carol over the garden wall, "have you been pinching my flowers again?"

No answer. So Carol repeated her accusation. Still no answer. She yelled even louder

"I said, have you been nicking my flowers?"

This time when she got no answer, she stormed round to her neighbour's house and found Beryl hanging out the washing at the side of the house.

"Didn't you hear me shouting," she said.

"No," replied Beryl innocently, "this wall must cut off the sound."

"Mmm," replied Carol, unconvinced. "Okay, I'll go back to my garden, you shout something to me and I'll see if I can hear it."

A moment later, Carol was back in her own garden and suddenly a voice shouted

"The old tart with the fancy flowers has been screwing around with the man from number 46."

Carol ran straight back round to Beryl's house and said breathlessly "You're right Beryl, I couldn't hear a thing. Anyway, I just wanted to say that anytime you'd like some flowers, feel free to help yourself."

★ ★ ★

Two women chatting over the garden wall.
"Hey, Myrtle, how come the weather's always fine when you hang your washing on the line. It never seems to get caught in the rain. What's your secret?"

Myrtle winked slyly and replied "It's all thanks to the old man. First thing in the morning I look at Ron in bed and if his dick is hanging to the left, then the weather will be fine. If it's hanging to the right, then it's going to rain."

"Mmm," replied her neighbour, "but what happens if it's standing to attention?"

"Oh my dear, if it's like that, then it's certainly not a day to do the washing!"

★ ★ ★

Marcia went round to Linda's for a cup of tea and a chat. As she looked round her kitchen, she remarked on all the modern, labour-saving devices that Linda had.

"Oh yes," replied Linda, "I get that from sex."

"Really?" replied Marcia, raising her eyebrows. "How come?"

"Well, I have a scale of charges. If my husband wants a quick feel, it'll cost him £1, if he wants to put his hand up my skirt, then it's £5 and so on, until the full thrust is £20. It's amazing how quickly the money builds up."

"What a great idea," said Marcia. "I'll have to try it with Charlie." They met up for their usual cup of tea the following Friday and Linda asked how it went.

"Hopeless," replied Marcia, blushing. "I charged him £1 for a quick fondle, but then I had to lend him £1 for another fondle and by that time, I was happy to pay £20 to get him into bed."

★ ★ ★

"Blimey," said Fred, as he met his drinking chums in the bar. "There was a right carry-on at our neighbour's house last night. Old Peter Parker – that daft, wouldn't say boo to a goose, bloke – came home early and found his wife in bed with the tennis coach. He shot 'em both dead."

"Bloody hell," came the reply.

"Well, it could have been worse," remarked Bill.

"How come?"

"If it had been last Tuesday, I'd be dead now."

★ ★ ★

"I haven't seen much of you these last few days," said June's neighbour. "Have you been busy?"

"Well, yes, I suppose you could say that," smiled June. "Ooh, I've got to tell someone," she continued. "I just can't believe what's happening. Last Tuesday morning, I'd just put the washing on the line when this young good looking man appeared. He asked me if Bernard was in and when I said "no", he took me inside, went up to the bedroom and made love to me, time and time again. I felt like a young girl. Anyway, that wasn't the end of it. Two days later, he came back asking for Bernard and when I told him he wasn't there, the man took me upstairs again and did the most wonderful things to me. And then this morning, he's waiting for me. Oh, I'm in seventh heaven! But there is one thing that puzzles me... why does he want to see Bernard?"

★ ★ ★

"Come in and have a cup of tea Mavis. You don't look so good," said her nosy neighbour.

"Oh thanks, Bet. No, I'm having a terrible time. It's Jim. I'm sure he's being unfaithful to me. Every day he's late home from work. He comes in with that silly grin on his face, stinking of perfume. Oh Bet, I've just about had enough. I've already lost nearly a stone in weight."

"Oh you poor dear," said Bet. "If I were you, I'd pack my bags and get out," she continued. "Find yourself a good lawyer and bleed him dry."

"Oh I will," replied Mavis, "but first I want to lose another stone."

★ ★ ★

Two snooty women, who couldn't stand the sight of each other, found themselves in the same railway carriage travelling up to London for the Chelsea Flower Show.

After thirty minutes of stony silence, one of the women spoke.

"How is your daughter getting on. I believe she works in London."

"Oh, she's a great success," crowed the other. "A beautiful flat in Mayfair, top of the range BMW, jewellery and furs... you name it, she's got it."

"Well! Well! Well!" replied the first woman. "That certainly rings a bell. My neighbour's daughter is a prostitute as well."

★ ★ ★

"What are you smiling for?" asked the woman's neighbour. "My husband's made me very happy," she replied. "He's just added some magic to our marriage... by disappearing."

★ ★ ★

Two neighbours talking over the garden wall.
"Your Jack's been away a long time Ethel."
"Yes, being a sailor keeps him away from home so much that by the time he comes home, I hardly recognise him."
"Oh dear, that's awful. What do you do?"
"I sleep with every man that comes to the house, just in case."

★ ★ ★

A woman was chatting to her neighbour at the garden gate. "My old man's getting very forgetful. These days I even have to follow him around to make sure he gets dressed properly. I've just asked him to pop down the shops for some milk and I bet he forgets. Oh dear," she sighed.

All of a sudden, they caught sight of her husband running up the road.

"Rita, Rita," he called breathlessly. "You'll never guess what's just happened. I helped this old eccentric man across the street and he gave me £1,000."

"You see," said the wife turning to her neighbour, "he's forgotten the milk!"

★ ★ ★

MEET THE NEWLY WEDS

The wedding had taken place in the outback and now the reception was in full flow. A couple of hours had passed when the bride's father called everyone to attention.

"Ladies, gentlemen and the rest of you. The wedding's off. We've run out of beer and er... oh yes, the bride's been raped by one of the guests."

A loud groan went up only to be followed by cheering a couple of minutes later.

"It's all right everyone," shouted the bride's father. "Problem over. Another 10 barrels of beer have arrived and the fella's said he's sorry."

★ ★ ★

The honeymoon couple were staying overnight at her mother's house before flying abroad the next day. They retired early, but less than five minutes later, the young girl raced back down the stairs.

"Oh mother," she said, "he's got such a hairy chest."

"That's quite normal," she replied, "now up you go and enjoy yourself."

But a minute later, she was back down again.

"Oh mother, he hasn't just got hair on his chest, it's all over his body."

"Come on girl, that's no problem, now get up there and show him what you're made of."

The young girl went back up to the bedroom just as her new husband was taking off his socks to reveal that part of his right foot was missing.

She ran downstairs again and squealed

"Mother, he's got three quarters of a foot."

"What!" exclaimed the woman, "you stay here and I'll go upstairs."

★ ★ ★

"My darling," he whispered on their honeymoon night. "I would travel to the ends of the earth for you, climb the highest mountain and swim the deepest sea."

Six months later she divorced him. He was never at home.

★ ★ ★

The morning after the honeymoon night, the young girl staggered down to breakfast looking stunned and exhausted. "My goodness!" exclaimed the owner of the hotel. "You look dead on your feet, haven't you just got married to that old bloke with the limp?"

"That's right," she said indignantly, "and he got me to marry him under false pretences. When he said he'd been saving up for 50 years, I thought he was talking about money."

★ ★ ★

A man couldn't decide who to marry. The beautiful young girl, full of fun, but a bit dumb, or the more mature plainer woman who was a famous opera singer. He eventually chose fame and fortune and went for the older woman. At breakfast on the morning after their wedding, he looked her up and down critically and said "Oh please sing, for goodness sake, sing."

★ ★ ★

To encourage her naive young husband to be more exciting in bed, the young wife bought a pair of crotchless knickers. At the time he was due home from work, she lay on the bed with her legs apart and said to him as he came through the door, "Hello darling, fancy a bit of this?"
"Agh! no thanks!" he said horrified. "Just look what it's done to your panties."

★ ★ ★

It was their honeymoon night and the new bride and her husband both had an awful secret. He suffered from very smelly feet and she had halitosis (dreadful bad breath). They prepared themselves for the wedding bed. He threw his socks in the bin and she ate a packet of mints. But it was no good, each of them knew they couldn't start their married life keeping secrets from each other. The man began "Darling, I have a confession to make. I suffer from smelly feet."
"It doesn't matter," she said bravely. "In fact I think I ought to tell you..."

But before she could say anymore, he interrupted her by saying "I know, I know, you're going to tell me you've swallowed my socks."

★ ★ ★

Poor Tracy! She'd only been married a few months but her husband, Dave, had already forsaken her for the pub. No matter how hard she tried – from wearing see-through nighties and provocative perfume – he would come in from work, get changed and disappear down the pub until the early hours of the morning. However all this changed one night when she heard him arrive home well before midnight. "Come on girl," he said, "get yourself upstairs and let's have all your clothes off."

Tracy could hardly believe it. At long last her husband had come home for a night of passion. She scampered up the stairs and stripped off.

"Right, now do a handstand," he said.

Anticipating wonderful things, Tracy did a handstand in front of the mirror. Dave then put his head between her legs and looking in the mirror, he remarked, "Yeah, perhaps the guys were right when they said a beard would suit me."

★ ★ ★

A young couple had been married for six months and one morning in bed, as the girl was fondling his manhood, she remarked "Oh Stevie, you said you were the only man to have one of these."

"That's right, darling," he whispered.

"But that can't be. I discovered yesterday, that your best friend has one as well."

The man thought quickly and replied "Well he's my best mate. I had a spare one, so I gave it to him."

"Oh Stevie, you are a silly!" she exclaimed. "You gave him the best one."

★ ★ ★

A man went to the doctor's, three weeks after getting married.

"I'm really fed up, doctor, my wife and I haven't consummated the marriage because she says it hurts too much. What can we do?"

"No need to get too worried," replied the doctor, "this problem is not uncommon. I suggest, before you start, to drop your manhood into a beaker of Vaseline."

"What!" exclaimed the man, "are you telling me you can get yours into a beaker!"

★ ★ ★

"Now see here, Dawn," said her husband of just five days. "We need to get something sorted out straight away."

He dropped his trousers and pointing to his todger said "If you want sex, pull on this once. If you don't want sex, pull on it 200 times."

★ ★ ★

A young woman, who'd only been married a month, went to the doctor's complaining of exhaustion.

"It's nothing to worry about," said the doctor. "It's not uncommon for newly weds to overdo their lovemaking. May I suggest that for the next month you confine your sexual activities to the days of the week which have an 's' in them. So that would be Tuesday, Wednesday, Thursday, Saturday and Sunday and the other two days you would rest."

So the girl went home and told her husband what the doctor had said and they agreed to follow his orders. Everything went according to plan the first week, but on the Monday night the husband woke up with a huge hard-on. He nudged his wife in the ribs to wake her up.

"What is it?" she yawned. "What day is it?"

"Monsday," he replied.

★ ★ ★

"What's wrong Cindy?" asked her mother when she saw her newly married daughter in floods of tears.

"Oh mum," she cried. "Stan's gone out shooting crap and I can't find out how to cook it in any of my recipe books."

★ ★ ★

Gerald decided to marry for a second time. He'd been a successful businessman and lived a very happy life but his wife of 35 years had died and he was lonely. For some time, he'd been dating a girl 20 years his junior and he felt the time was right to pop the question.

"We..ll," she hesitated. "There are a few things I'd insist upon."

"Just name them, my dear," he replied.

"First of all, I'd want my own monthly account."

"It's yours," he replied.

"And I'd like my own car."

"Certainly," he said.

She paused for a moment and then said "And what about sex?"

"Oh infrequently," he replied, blushing.

She mused on this for a moment or two and then continued, "Is that one word or two?"

★ ★ ★

A man kept begging his girlfriend to marry him, but he was a lazy swine and wouldn't get up off his arse to go and find work.

"How can I marry you?" she would ask. "What would we live on?"

"Love, my darling, love," he would always reply.

Eventually he wore her down and she agreed to marry him. On the evening of their wedding he walked in to find her sitting naked on the electric fire.

"What are you doing!" he exclaimed.

"Just heating your dinner," she replied sweetly.

★ ★ ★

A naive young girl was taking the library trolley around the hospital wards when she noticed a man who had his penis heavily bandaged.

"Oh you poor thing," she remarked. "Did you break a bone?"

"A bone!" he replied astonished. "Are you married?"

"Oh yes," she said blushing. "We've been married for three months."

"Well in that case, you've certainly married quite a stud," he replied.

★ ★ ★

Three honeymoon couples end up at the same hotel and after the girls have gone to prepare for bed, the men get talking and boasting about their sexual prowess. They agree to swap stories the following morning. The next morning, the first man describes his amazing night of passion.

"Five times we did it," he said, "and I'm ready to go again tonight."

"Well, it was seven times for us," said the second man. "She couldn't get enough of me."

They turned to the third man and said, "So how about you?"

"Well, we made love just once."

"Only once? What did your wife say?"

"It'll soon be breakfast time, I think we ought to try and grab some sleep."

★ ★ ★

When the husband walked into the bedroom, the morning after their wedding, he found his naive young wife in floods of tears.

"Darling, what's wrong. Didn't you enjoy last night?" he asked.

"Oh, I enjoyed it very much," she cried, "but look at it now, it's all used up."

★ ★ ★

A Scotsman was marrying an English girl and mindful that he didn't want to upset the guests south of the border, he decided to wear something under his kilt. He went along to the outfitters and bought six yards of his own tartan which were to be made up into some special underpants. The day before the wedding, the pants were ready and delivered to his home.

"You bought too much," said the seamstress, so there's three yards over which you can keep until you need it."

The day of the wedding dawned. The Scotsman was unbelievably nervous. So much so, that he forgot to put on his brand new underpants. Anyway, it didn't matter. The day was a great success. That night, once the festivities were over, the newly married couple retired to the honeymoon suite. The groom was fairly drunk by this time and lifted his kilt high in the air to show his new wife the special tartan underpants - forgetting that he hadn't put them on that morning.

"What do you reckon to that?" he said proudly. "I bet you've not seen anything like that before?"

She gasped with delight at his impressive tackle.

"Oh lovely!" she said.

The groom smiled with satisfaction.

"Well, there's another three yards of this at home which you can use when we return."

★ ★ ★

The young newlyweds rushed down to the station and just caught the train as it was leaving the platform.

"Phew! That was close," remarked the bridegroom. "I hope we've got everything."

A few moments later, the ticket inspector arrived.

"Tickets please, everyone," he called.

The bridegroom hastily pulled out a piece of paper and handed it to the inspector.

"I'm sorry," said the inspector, noticing the confetti all over their clothes, "but although this piece of paper allows you a lifetime of free rides, it's not valid on the 4.42 to Edinburgh. You see sir," he said, handing back the paper, "this is your marriage certificate."

★ ★ ★

Chris and Lucy had been courting for three years but they'd never been intimate because he had a wooden leg and could never tell her about it. They decided to get married and on the momentous day, Chris realised he was going to have to tell Lucy the truth, but still he chickened out. That night, when they got into the bedroom, Chris turned to Lucy and said

"Lucy, darling, I've got a big secret and I guess it's time I told you what it was."

With that, he switched off the light, stripped off, and detached his wooden leg.

"Here," he whispered, handing her the leg.

"Oooh," she chuckled. "You old devil, now this is what I call a surprise."

★ ★ ★

A couple from the back-to-back houses in Leeds had just got married and for the first time ever, they were spending the honeymoon night in a very posh hotel in London. The following morning, they came down to breakfast in the sumptuous dining room where it soon became obvious that other couples had also spent their honeymoon night in the hotel. Harold was determined not to let himself down, so he listened carefully to the conversations around him in an attempt to pick up some social graces. Behind him, he heard the man say to his wife

THE BEST ADULT JOKE BOOK EVER

"Oh sugar, pass the sugar please."
Then to his left, he heard another man say
"Pass the honey, honey."
"Okay," he thought, "now I know how to act." So he turned
to his new wife and whispered lovingly, "pass the bacon, pig."

★ ★ ★

The new wife approached her husband timidly and said in a
faltering voice
"Oh Scot, these first two months of our married life have been
wonderful. I couldn't ask for a more thoughtful and loving man.
Except... er... there's just something that's bothering me.
"Come on love, let's have no worries between us, he replied.
"Well, you're always picking your nose, and we always make
love with you on top."
"Oh, I can easily explain that," he replied.
"When I was young, my father gave me two pieces of advice
which I've always tried to follow. He said 'Keep your nose clean
and don't fuck up.'"

★ ★ ★

MEET THE NYMPHS

A priest went to see sweet Mary O'Sullivan who was in hospital for appendicitis.

"Hello Mary, I prayed for you last night," he said.

"Oh there's no need for that," she replied. "Just look me up in the phone directory."

★ ★ ★

What's a nymphomaniac's great dilemma?
Meeting a man with V.D. who has got an enormous dick.

★ ★ ★

A nymphomaniac went to buy her latest boyfriend some cricket equipment.

"How much are the stumps?" she asked.

"£15 Miss."

"And the bat?"

"£20."

"Well I can only afford one, so I'll take the bat."

"How about a ball for the bat," persisted the pushy salesman.

"No thanks," she replied, "but I'll blow you for the stumps."

★ ★ ★

A 'good time' girl went up to a man leaning on the bar and whispered in his ear

"Hey, big boy, I'm all yours for just £100."

"Blimey, that's a lot of money," the man replied.

"Yeah, but for that you get anything and everything you desire," she cooed, pressing her voluptuous body against his. "And I mean anything!"

She saw he was getting interested so she continued

"Yes, any fantasy you like, come on, just whisper three little words in my ear and it'll be done for just £100."

"Just £100," he mused.

He thought for a moment and then said, "Decorate the house."

★ ★ ★

It was almost a disaster when the blonde accidentally made two dates on the same night.

But it was all right in the end... she managed to squeeze both of them in.

★ ★ ★

Two 'good time' girls were preparing for their night on the town.

"Hey Marcia," said Jane, watching her friend walk across the room with her legs wide apart. "What's this strange walk all about?"

"I've got a really hot date later this evening and I've put my hair in curlers," she replied.

★ ★ ★

What do you get when you cross a nymphomaniac with a Dry Cleaning specialist?
Someone who'll suck your laundry.

★ ★ ★

"You just wouldn't believe it," said the dumb blonde to her friend. "Men always assume you're going to spend the night with them. I'm sick of it. Take last night for example. I was over at this bloke's flat and he took it for granted I was stopping. Well! that was the last straw, I was so insulted, I put my dress back on and left."

★ ★ ★

A young girl, not inexperienced in the ways of sex, was browsing through the big department store when she spotted the most beautiful pair of shoes she'd ever seen.
"Oh, I must have them," she said to herself, but the price was outrageous. However, not discouraged she sought out the manager who happened to be a young buck in his 30's and thought he was God's gift to women. It wasn't long before they came to an agreement that she would have the shoes in return for a few favours in the storeroom.
"I'll soon have you screaming with delight," he boasted.
They went into the back, he proudly revealed his todger and off they went. But no matter how much effort he put into it, she

hardly reacted. She just lay there looking at her prize shoes lying at her side. Now the man's pride was at stake, so he went at it for a second time. But he still didn't get the reaction he was looking for. So he tried a third time and to his immense relief, she began to move, lifting her legs higher and grabbing him tighter around the neck.

"That's my boy," he said to himself and then smugly remarked to the girl, "You see, I told you it would be the best you've ever had."

"Oh, don't be daft," she replied. "I'm just trying on my new shoes."

★ ★ ★

What does a nymphomaniac say after sex?
Thanks guys.

★ ★ ★

Simon had such a bad throat, he could hardly speak. So he decided to pop round to the doctor's surgery.

He knocked at the door and it was opened by the doctor's beautiful young daughter.

"Is he in?" he whispered.

"No," she whispered, looking around. "Come on in."

★ ★ ★

Why is a nymphomaniac like a doorknob?
Everyone gets a turn.

★ ★ ★

What happens when a group of nymphomaniacs have a party?
Everybody comes.

★ ★ ★

What's the four letter word a nymphomaniac usually
screams out during sex?
Next.

★ ★ ★

The nymphomaniac looked at the strapping young man and said
"Hey, big boy, can you make love to me and hurt me?"
"Sure can," he said.
So he fucked her and then hit her over the head with a
blunt instrument.

★ ★ ★

A nymphomaniac is out to have a good time and meets up
with three blokes in the local nightclub. She can't decide
which one to make a play for, but noticing they all stutter, she
devises a plan.

"Look chaps," she says. "If one of you can tell me where you come from, without stuttering, I'll give them a blow job."

The lads agree enthusiastically.

"I come from Leeeeds," says the first.

"Oh shame," she says.

"I come from Birminghhham," says the second.

"Never mind," she replies.

"I come from London ...."

"Great," she says and in a flash has his willy out of his trousers. But just as she's about to perform he says "ddderry."

★ ★ ★

MEET THE PARENTS

The man had been working on the oil rig for three months but now he had a two week break.

"I can't wait to get home," he said, "before the kids forget what I look like."

His pessimistic workmate replied

"Just make sure you know who they look like!"

★ ★ ★

"You may scoff son," said the father, "but wisdom comes with age. Consider this: A young bull will spot a herd of cows on the other side of the field and rush right over, giving a couple of them a right seeing to. But an old bull will take his time, walk over slowly and fuck the lot."

★ ★ ★

The delicatessen owner was very sad that his forty-year-old daughter had never married. In fact, she didn't even have a boyfriend because she said she wasn't interested. Then one night, her father heard a noise in the shop and creeping down to investigate he spied his daughter masturbating with a large German sausage. The next day, a customer walked into the shop and asked for a selection of cheeses.

"Oh, I'll also have some of that German sausage," he said.

"I'm sorry, sir," came the reply, "that's not for sale, that's my son-in-law."

★ ★ ★

For the fifth time that week, Jane had arrived home at two in the morning looking very dishevelled. Her parents knew she had an exciting new boyfriend, but her appearance was causing them great concern.

"Janey, Janey," they said the next morning, "this new boyfriend – what's he like? What are his intentions?"

"I don't know," she replied, "he keeps me mostly in the dark."

★ ★ ★

The tight-fisted couple asked their son what he wanted for his birthday.

"I wanna watch," he replied.

So they let him.

★ ★ ★

The angry father opened the door to find his daughter canoodling in the porch with her boyfriend.

"It's nearly half past one in the morning," he bellowed, "do you think you can stay here all night."

"Gosh, I don't know," replied the boyfriend. "I'll have to ring my parents for permission."

★ ★ ★

"How did you get on at school today?" dad asks his son.

"Okay," he replies. "We had a really hard spelling test, they were such long words."

"Really? Such as?"

"Masturbation," says the boy.

"My goodness!" exclaims dad, "that is a mouthful."

"No dad," corrects the boy. "A mouthful is a blow job, masturbation is done with the hand."

★ ★ ★

While his mother was in the kitchen cooking dinner, her young son was playing with his toy garage. For a while, all was quiet and then she heard him say "Call yourself a bloody mechanic, this fucking car has broken down again."

Then later she overheard him shout "Hey, you! Get your arse over here and look at this engine."

"Johnny, Johnny," she said, coming into the room. "Enough of that dreadful language. I won't have you talk like that, now go to your room."

An hour passed and mum let Johnny come back down and continue playing. She smiled as she heard him say "Bay number 5, sir? That'll be £10 please. Yes, you'll find the car wash around the back. Have a nice day... Oh, good morning madam, I'm afraid your car isn't ready yet. If you want to know why, go and ask that bloody cow in the kitchen."

★ ★ ★

A father decided to test his 18-year-old son's initiative. He gave him a duck and told him to go into town and come back better off. On his travels, the son met a prostitute and asked for 15 minutes of her time in return for the duck. It was an unusual request, but she accepted and took him back to her flat. After the session, the prostitute was so impressed with his athleticism that she told him she'd give the duck back if they did it again. So later that day, he still had the duck and he'd enjoyed himself a great deal. Then to his dismay, the duck was frightened by a loud noise. It flew into the path of an oncoming truck and was killed instantly. The driver was so upset he gave the boy £10 compensation.

"So how did it go," asked the father when his son arrived home.

"Pretty good," replied the son.

"I got a fuck for a duck, a duck for a fuck and £10 for a fucked up duck."

★ ★ ★

A discontented woman had taken her small son for a walk in the woods, but within moments of her looking away, the boy had wandered off. She searched for him for over an hour and it was beginning to grow dark. As a last resort, she looked heavenwards and cried

"Oh God, please don't let anything happen to my son, please take me instead."

Moments later, she heard crying and there caught in some undergrowth, was her little son.

"Oh thank you, thank you," she said happily, running up to him. Then suddenly she stopped and remarked, "But just before you go, God, he did have his teddy bear with him!"

★ ★ ★

A father is keen to take his son for an aeroplane ride but the only person he knows who will do it is a rather shady stuntman. The stuntman is always looking for a way to make easy money so he suggests that they can have the ride free as long as they don't say anything or make a noise. If they do, then they will have to pay double.

The father agrees and tells his son there must be complete silence or the pilot will not fly.

The next day, the trip takes place and very soon the small plane is soaring high into the sky. The stuntman smiles to himself, certain that once he begins to perform some of his incredible manoeuvres, one of them is sure to make a noise.

He loops the loop, flies upside-down, drops like a stone from a great height and many other tricks over the 30 minute period. But not a sound is uttered.

Eventually, admitting defeat, he returns to base.

"That was quite amazing," he says to the father, shaking his hand." I was sure one of you would have broken the silence."

"It was very hard," admits the father, "particularly when my son fell out halfway through the trip."

★ ★ ★

As the young girl passed her parents' bedroom she saw them both changing to go out. Her father had just come out of the shower and was drying himself.

"Oh mama!" she cried "What's that?" pointing to her father's well-endowed tackle.

"Ah ha," smiled Mum, "that's something very special."

"Indeed," interrupted her father, "if it wasn't for this you wouldn't be here... Come to think of it, neither would I!"

★ ★ ★

The man at the bar looked sadly into his pint of beer and sighed heavily.

"What's up Bob?" asked the landlord. "It's not like you to be so down in the mouth."

"It's my four-year-old son" he said "The little bugger's got our next-door neighbour pregnant."

"Get away!" exclaimed the landlord. "That's impossible."
"It's not. He punctured all my condoms with a needle."

★ ★ ★

John had been put over his father's knee and given a couple of sharp taps on the backside for swearing at his mum.
"Right son," said Dad sternly, "now tell me why I did that."
"Bloody hell!" replied the boy astonished. "First you whack me and then you don't know why the fuck you did it."

★ ★ ★

"Now son," said his father. "Let's see how much you've learnt in maths. What's two and two."
After a moment the boy replied "Four."
"Good," replied his father, "but let's try and be a little quicker. What's four and four?"
This time the boy counted out the numbers on his fingers and replied "Eight."
"Okay," said dad patiently, "but try not to use your fingers. Put your hands in your pockets. Now, what's five and five."
After a few moments of fumbling the boy replied "Eleven."

★ ★ ★

"Dad," said the young teenager pointing to the different-sized packets of condoms, "Why do they come in different amounts?"

"Well son," replied his dad, "the pack of three is for the lad who gets lucky at the weekends when he goes out clubbing. One for Friday and two for Saturday. Now the pack of six is for the experienced young bachelor who has a date nearly every day of the week. And finally, the pack of 12 is for the married man. One for each month, January, February, March..."

★ ★ ★

"Geraldine, how could you!?" exclaimed her mother, looking at paintings of her naked daughter hanging on the studio wall.
"I can't believe you'd pose nude for your boyfriend."
"Oh mother, I didn't," she replied. "He must have painted them from memory."

★ ★ ★

Two hillbillies decide it's time to teach their 20-year-old son about sex.
"Come here, Arnie," calls Pa. "Come into the bedroom, there's something we want to show you."
Arnie shuffles into the bedroom to be greeted by the sight of his parents standing before him stark naked.
"It's time you learnt about sex, so your Ma and I are going to show you. See this hole between your Ma's legs, well watch carefully."
To the boy's astonishment, he watches open-mouthed as his

parents get it together on the bed in front of him. Just then, his younger brother walks by and wants to know what all the noise is about.

"Ma and Pa are showing me what sex is," replies Arnie.

"What's sex?" asks Colin.

"Look, I'll show you. See that hole in Pa, now watch this!"

★ ★ ★

MEET THE PERCY

What do you call a group of twelve men with large willies?
A hung jury.

★ ★ ★

What do you call a man with a 4" penis?
Norm.

★ ★ ★

The arrogant man had been thrusting away madly for more than five minutes when his date for the night turned to him and said
"You remind me of Valentino."
"The great lover, you mean," he said smugly... "but isn't he dead?"
"Exactly," she replied.

★ ★ ★

An arrogant man was walking in the park when he saw a pretty girl approaching with her dog.
"Hello darling," said 'god's gift to women.'
"'Nice day for it," he added, winking.

The girl ignored him but the dog got an erection.

Puzzled, the man engineered another meeting with her a few minutes later and the dog reacted in the same way.

"Hey, what's going on here?" he asked. "Why's your dog getting so frisky every time I talk to you."

"Easy," she replied haughtily, "he knows guys like you are all cocksuckers!"

★ ★ ★

"Come on girl," whispered the boastful man, "how about coming back to my place and letting me give you six inches."

"No thanks," she replied. "Looking at you, I don't think you've got the energy to get it up three times."

★ ★ ★

As she left the room, the sweet young girl said to her boss

"Oh just one more thing Mr Arno, you've left the barrack doors open."

It wasn't until much later that he understood what she meant when he looked down and realised he'd left his flies undone. He pressed the intercom and said "Maureen, can you come in here for a moment please?"

As she walked in he said proudly

"When I left the barrack doors open this morning, did you see a soldier standing to attention?"

"Oh no," she replied sweetly. "I saw a shell-shocked veteran who'd seen better days."

★ ★ ★

An arrogant man asked his wife if she would like some ice cream he'd bought back from the supermarket.
"How hard is it?" she asked.
"About as hard as my dick," he boasted.
"Okay, pour me some then."

★ ★ ★

A husband and wife are admiring their newborn baby son.
"My goodness, just look at the size of his willy," said dad proudly.
"Yes sweetheart," answered his wife, "but at least he's got your nose."

★ ★ ★

A man goes to the doctor's because his penis is a massive 60 inches long.
"It's ruining my life," complained the man. "Is there anything you can do?"
"I'm sorry, there isn't," said the doctor, "but I think I have an answer to your problem. I've heard there's a deep pond in the middle of Crossways Wood. When you find it, you will see a frog sitting on a lily pad. You must ask it to marry you and when it says no, your penis will shorten by 10 inches."
However absurd the story, the man is so desperate, he sets out for the wood. Sure enough, there's a frog sitting on the lily pad.

"Hey frog," he shouts, "will you marry me?"

"No," replies the frog and the man's penis shrinks by 10 inches.

The man is overcome with happiness. Two more times he asks the frog to marry him and it shrinks another 20 inches. Wonderful, thinks the man, just once more and it'll be perfect.

"Hey froggy, will you marry me?"

By this time the frog is so annoyed with all the pestering that he shouts back

"I'm fed up with telling you, no, no and no again!"

★ ★ ★

A male visitor to a country golf club ended up in the female locker room by mistake. He was unaware of this mix up until halfway through his shower when two ladies entered and he could hear them talking across the way. In a panic, all he could think of was to escape without being recognised. He wrapped a towel round his head and in a sudden dash, ran naked from the room.

"My goodness," exclaimed the first woman. "That certainly wasn't my husband."

"Nor mine," said the second.

"In fact," continued the first, "he's not even a member of this club."

★ ★ ★

The woman's husband had been chosen as opening batsman for the local cricket team. She was so concerned he might injure himself that she immediately went out to buy him a box for protection.

"What size would that be?" asked the young saleswoman. "They come in different sizes."

"Well, I'm not sure," replied the woman blushing.

"Okay, no problem," replied the assistant, holding up her little finger. "What about this?"

"Oh no, bigger," replied the wife.

The assistant held up two fingers.

"No, bigger than that," came the reply.

Eventually, she held up all five fingers.

"Yes, that's it," said the wife triumphantly.

So the assistant put all five fingers in her mouth and declared with some expertise, "Fine, that's a size 4 then."

★ ★ ★

Marvin went into the chemist for a packet of condoms but when the girl asked him what size he needed, he shook his head in bewilderment.

"I've no idea," he said.

"Oh that's no problem," replied the girl kindly. "If you'd just like to come in the back with me a moment."

Once there, she took off her knickers and asked him to enter her. He was astonished but delighted.

"You're a size 4," she said after a moment. "Now please take it out."

They went back into the shop and he bought a packet of size 4.

On his way home, he bumped into his sleazy friend Maurice, and recounted his amazing experience.

"Cor! I need a bit of that!" sleazed Maurice and off he went looking for the chemist.

"A packet of condoms please, Miss," he said, moments later.

"Certainly sir, what size?"

"Oh, I don't know," said Marvin.

"Okay, if you'd like to come in the back with me."

He did as she asked and he received the same service.

"You're a size 5," she said. "Now take it out please. How many packets do you want?"

But sleazy Marvin refused to stop until he was completely satisfied, and then zipping himself up he said to her grinning "I don't want any today, I only came in for a fitting."

★ ★ ★

"I'm afraid, Mr Smallman, that tests have shown your penis is going to get bigger and thicken up," said the specialist.

"Well, that sounds all right to me," replied the man smiling. "But why?"

"It's going to do this because you have a rare disease. And then...er...it's going to drop off."

★ ★ ★

A woman went to an alternative healer to find out if anything could be done to make her breasts bigger.

"No problem," said the healer. "All you have to do is recite 'Mary, Mary quite contrary' and you will soon notice the difference."

Walking through the park on the way home, the girl couldn't stop thinking about the amazing treatment and sitting down on a bench, she started to recite the verse. All of a sudden, a man appeared behind her and said "I bet I know where you've been," and he began to recite, "Hickory, dickory, dock..."

★ ★ ★

The year was 2900 and advances in medicine had resulted in special body part shops appearing all round the country. One morning, a young man walked into one of these shops and requested a new penis.

"What size sir?" came the reply. "We have 6-inch, 8-inch and 10-inch."

As the man looked at the different sizes he remarked "Haven't you got the 10-inch in white?"

★ ★ ★

MEET THE
PLEASURE SEEKERS

The hunting expedition had travelled further into the mountains than anyone had gone before. On the third day, they were confronted by a small group of savages.

"Take cover," yelled the expedition leader, "and get me my red jacket." It was only a small skirmish and the hunters quickly saw off the retreating savages.

A few days later, they were confronted by a larger band of savages and again the leader shouted out, "Okay men, shoot at will, and can someone get my red jacket."

The hunters fought bravely and were finally victorious, sustaining only two minor injuries.

That night round the campfire, they talked over the week's events. "Thanks to our leader, we've defeated the enemy every time. It won't be long before we reach our destination and we'll be famous."

"Here's to Bob," and they drank a celebratory toast.

"By the way, Bob, just out of interest, why do you always ask for your red jacket as we go into battle?"

Bob replied "If I wear the red jacket and get wounded, no one will see the blood and lose confidence."

The men were very impressed. They continued their journey to the heart of the mountains but disaster struck the following evening. As they came over a high ridge, they were confronted by a band of savages, at least 500 in number.

"Fight for your lives," yelled Bob, "and will someone get me my brown trousers."

★ ★ ★

A millionaire had been going out with a waitress for two months. They'd had a great time, often out until the early hours of the morning, but both of them knew nothing serious would come of it.
Then one evening the waitress turned to the man and said "Why don't we get married?"
The man looked shocked, "Oh come on Rose, you know that's not possible, when I marry it has to be to a titled family."
"I know," she sighed.
"Then why did you ask?"
"I just wanted to know how it felt to lose a fortune."

★ ★ ★

A party of game shooters stopped overnight at an hotel in the middle of Dartmoor. They'd had a very successful day so were in the mood to celebrate and by the time they retired to bed, many were unsteady on their feet.

Charles staggered into his room and was just about to collapse on the bed when he realised he hadn't cleaned his gun for the next day's shooting. As he sat down to the task, his befuddled mind didn't realise it was still loaded and all of a sudden the gun fired a bullet which went straight through the ceiling. The following day at breakfast, the manager came up to him quite upset.

"I hear you had an accident with your gun last night. In fact it went straight through the ceiling and into the room of a young honeymoon couple, badly damaging the man's finger."

"What!" exclaimed Charles, "that's a damned poor show. Do convey to them my sincere apologies."

Then after a moment's pause, Charles continued "Still it could have been worse, had it been a Frenchman, I would've shot his head off."

★ ★ ★

A man was very embarrassed about having a wooden leg and a bald head so when he received an invitation to a fancy dress ball, he panicked because he didn't want people to notice his problems. His friend advised him to write to a fancy dress company and explain his dilemma. A few days later, a huge parcel arrived and on opening it, he found a pirate's outfit. The enclosed letter informed him that the spotted handkerchief would hide his bald head and the wooden leg would be ideal for him to take on the character of Long John Silver. The man was outraged and wrote a strong letter back complaining that all they had done was draw even more attention to his wooden leg.

Some time later another parcel arrived, this time it contained a monks habit. The enclosed letter informed him that the habit would hide his leg and the bald head would fit the part perfectly. The man wrote an even angrier letter back,

pointing out that now the costume would emphasise his bald head. By return of post he received a small packet and a note which read

"We enclose a tin of treacle. We suggest you pour this over your bald head, stick your wooden leg up your arse and go as a toffee apple."

★ ★ ★

A man walked into a restaurant and asked the waiter for a bowl of chilli.

"I'm sorry sir, we've run out," replied the waiter. "The customer on the next table had the last helping."

Disappointed, the man ordered a coffee only and as he sat drinking it, he noticed the man on the next table had not touched his chilli but was eating a steak instead. So he leaned over and said

"Excuse me, are you going to eat that chilli?"

"No mate," came the reply, "you're welcome to have it."

Delighted, the man tucked into his chilli and had eaten half of it when he noticed a severed rat lying on the bottom of the bowl. Shocked at the disgusting sight, he retched and puked up the chilli he'd eaten back into the bowl. At this, the man on the next table remarked "Yeah, that's about as far as I got too."

★ ★ ★

An Englishman walked into a French restaurant and ordered a bowl of soup, but when it arrived there was a dead fly floating in it. He called the waiter back and spoke to him in French.
"Pardon, regardez le mouche."
The waiter replied "Not le mouche, monsieur, la mouche."
"Good gracious!" exclaimed the man, "you must have wonderful eyesight."

★ ★ ★

It was the night of the summer ball and all those attending were dressed in their very best. DJ's for the men, evening gowns for the women.

Halfway through the event, Alistair noticed a young woman sitting on her own, so liking what he saw, he strolled over to ask her for a dance.

"Thank you for asking," she said, "but I'm afraid I shall have to say no, because I have no legs."

The man was terribly embarrassed but she was so sweet, he sat down next to her and the rest of the evening passed in pleasant conversation.

"Would you mind if I took you home?" he said much later, and she quickly took up his offer.

When they arrived at her house, he kissed her goodnight and was surprised to find how passionately she returned his advances. It wasn't long before he was completely carried away with the situation and he whispered to her urgently "How much I would like to make love to you! But this car is too awkward and I don't know how we'd manage."

"Oh, that's no problem," she replied. "Under my dress there's a big hook strapped to my back. If you place that over the top of the garden fence, I'm sure it would work."

So he carried her over to the fence and they were soon in the throes of extreme passion.

Now Alistair was quite a decent bloke and after it was all over, he felt somewhat ashamed of his behaviour. He took her down from the fence and carried her into the house.

"I'm awfully sorry," he said, "I feel a bit of a heel."

"Oh not at all," she assured him. "You've been the perfect gentleman. Most of the others usually leave me hanging from the fence."

★　★　★

After a long and tiring day's hunting in the jungle, the group of men made their way back to the camp for their evening meal. That night they had plenty to celebrate, having shot some good trophies, so they laid into the whisky quite heavily. At one point, Martin staggered off to have a pee and being so drunk he failed to do his fly up again. As he sat down, Gerry turned to him and said

"Hey, Martin, I just saw a big snake in that chair when you sat down."

"Really?" he replied, somewhat dazed.

"Yes, I can still see it. Keep still and I'll knock it on the head with this empty bottle."

Thump, there was an almighty thwack which brought tears to Martin's eyes.

"Quick man," he said, "do it again, the bugger's just bitten me."

★ ★ ★

Two spinsters went on holiday together and once they'd booked into the hotel, they made their way down to the beach. As one went to dip her toes in the water, the other noticed a man sitting on his own. He'd obviously just arrived because he was deathly pale. Plucking up courage, she went over to talk to him.

"Hi, I'm Mildred. Have you just arrived, you look rather pale?"

"Yeah," he snarled. "I've been inside for the past 15 years."

"Oh really? What for?"

"Five years for burglary, two years for deception..."

"Oh my!" she exclaimed.

"...and the last eight years for killing my wife."

Mildred's face brightened and she called over to her friend, "Hey Flo, he's single."

★ ★ ★

A man walked into a massage parlour and was taken to a small room told to undress and lie face down on the bed. He'd just done this when a beautiful blonde entered the room, dressed in a shimmering, but skimpy bikini, her massive breasts threatening to fall out of her bra at any moment. As he lay there, she covered him with sweet smelling oils and gently rubbed down his body.

Unable to control himself, he was soon sporting a huge erection and as she asked him to turn over, it was revealed in all it's glory.

"I see sir may want to do something about that," she said smiling, as she walked seductively out of the door.

He lay there in a state of ecstasy. Any minute she'd return and administer to his every need. She'd probably gone to change into another little sexy number.

Five minutes later she opened the door and said gently, "Have you finished now?"

★ ★ ★

Driving through a rough part of town, the young couple's car broke down and the man set out to look for the nearest garage.

"But what about me?" asked his wife, looking scared. "If you leave me here alone, I might get raped."

"Don't worry," he reassured her. "Just tell them you were on your way to the clap clinic."

★ ★ ★

The skinflint looked at the high prices on the menu with shock. Thinking quickly, he turned to his girlfriend and said "What would you like my little plump one?"

★ ★ ★

As the Jewish boy and his girlfriend canoodled on the back seat of the car, she turned to him and said
"That's odd. You don't feel Jewish."

★ ★ ★

Girls. Always remember when a man boasts about his manhood, a 10" willy is a rule not an exception.

★ ★ ★

The horse fair had come to town and as Beth showed her city cousin the ways of the country, she pointed to the horse up for sale and remarked
"I wouldn't bid for him. He's not the best. For a start, he's hung like a man."

★ ★ ★

What's the difference between 'Oooh' and 'Aaah?'
About four inches.

★ ★ ★

A word of advice to the girls.
Never judge a man's horse power by the size of his exhaust.

★ ★ ★

It's a well known fact that if you go out with a man in tight trousers, and he finds them comfortable, then you'll never be happy... there'll be nothing in them to satisfy you.

★ ★ ★

On their second date, the couple drive to lovers' lane and climb into the back seat.

"Don't worry," he says. "I've got a packet of condoms here. They're flavoured ones."

A moment later she cries

"Mmm, that's nice. Salt and vinegar."

"Hold on," he replies. "I haven't got it on yet."

★ ★ ★

Did you hear about the well endowed father who took part in his son's sports day activities?

He won the three-legged race all by himself.

★ ★ ★

Three rats meet up in the underground sewer and start boasting about their toughness.

"I'm not scared of anything," says the first, "I'll raid any house, take what I want and they never catch me."

"That's nothing," replies the second scornfully. "Whenever I see rat poison I just chew it up and spit it out."

They wait for the third to speak but he gets up and starts to move away.
"Hey, what's up, where are you going?"
He replies haughtily
"I ain't got time for this, I'm off to fuck the cat."

★ ★ ★

"Hey Mary, I hear your boyfriend is well hung."
"Mmm," she replied, "he buys his socks in packets of three."

★ ★ ★

MEET THE PROPER CHARLIES

Did you hear about the simple man who was determined to have a good night on the town but instead spent the whole night in a warehouse?

★ ★ ★

"Aagh, I shouldn't have had that vindaloo last night," said Jack, as he felt pains shoot through his stomach. As fast as he could, he headed for the public conveniences, rushed in and sat down in the first cubicle.

"That's better," he said, happily, but then looking down, he noticed two pairs of shoes.

"Oh well," he cried, jumping up quickly. "So sorry mate, it was a bit of an emergency, I didn't see you sitting there."

"No harm done," replied the man.

"When I saw you were about to sit down, I pulled your trousers up again."

★ ★ ★

A travelling salesman stops overnight at a city hotel. As he's waiting to book in, he notices a woman giving him the eye from across the foyer.

"I'm in here," he thinks as he saunters over to speak to her. Moments later, he returns to the receptionist and says

"Make that a double room, please, my wife is going to join me." After a busy night, the man bids farewell to his bed companion and goes to pay the bill.

"That'll be £350 please," she says.

"What!?" he exclaims, "but I've only been here one night."

"Yes sir, but your wife's been here all week."

★ ★ ★

Three lads from the country were visiting the big city but on their first night, they were held up by a mugger.

"Give me all your money," he demanded, "or I'll inject you with AIDS," he said, brandishing a needle.

Two of the lads immediately handed over their money but the third refused and so the mugger stuck the needle in him and then ran away.

"Larry," gasped the other two, "don't you realise what you've done? That man's injected you with AIDS."

"No, it's all right lads," he said, smiling, "I'm wearing a condom."

★ ★ ★

Two hunters are walking through the jungle, one is carrying a concrete post and the other is carrying a wooden shed.

"Why have you got that shed with you?" asks the first hunter.

He replies

"Well you see, if we get attacked by a wild animal, I can take refuge inside the shed."

They walk on a bit and the second hunter enquires.

"So why are you carrying a concrete post?"

"Well, if we get confronted by a wild animal, I can drop the post so I can run faster."

★ ★ ★

The weather had turned very cold and as a naive young girl was waiting on the platform for the train to arrive, her hands and feet started to go numb. Looking around, she noticed people putting their hands between their legs and when she did the same, her hands warmed up nicely. The following week, the weather was still very cold on the night she went out on her first date. Walking back through the park, they sat down on a park bench and feeling cold, the girl put her hands between her legs. When the boy asked her what she was doing she explained and he told her his hands were cold as well. So in all innocence she put his hands between her legs and said

"There, doesn't that feel better?"

"Oh yes," he said nodding enthusiastically. A short while later he complained his nose was feeling cold so she warmed him up again. Then later still, he told her his willy was so cold it had gone stiff...

The next day, her mates asked here how the date had gone.

"Fine," she replied, "but it was such a cold night. Did you realise that when men's willies thaw out, they make an awful mess?"

★ ★ ★

Two hillbillies were visiting the big city for the first time and ended up in a big department store. They were 'gob smacked' by everything around them particularly two silver coloured doors which seemed to open and close on their own. As they watched, a wizened old lady pressed a button on the wall and as the doors opened she entered and the doors closed again. Lots of lights started flashing and some moments later, the doors reopened and a beautiful young woman stepped out.

"Well, I'll be damned," remarked one of the hillbillies. "I'm off to get the wife."

★ ★ ★

Three men, an Englishman, an Italian and an Irishman are trapped on the roof of a burning building. Below them on the road, the firemen are holding out a blanket for them to jump into.

"Come on," they yell to the Englishman, "jump!"

So he jumps and just as he's about to reach the blanket, they pull it away and he lands on the pavement, stone dead.

"Come on," shout the firemen to the Italian, "hurry up and jump."

"Oh no," screams the Italian, "you'll take the blanket away."

"No we won't. That bloke was a nasty criminal. We'll keep it here for you."

So the Italian jumps and again the blanket is removed so he falls to his death.

"Right, come on," they call to the Irishman, "let's have you."

"Holy Mary," shouts the Irishman. "You won't trick me like that. I know you'll take the blanket away."

"No, no," and again they urge him to jump.

"It doesn't matter what you say, I don't believe you," he replies, "so I want you to back away slowly and leave the blanket where it is on the ground."

★ ★ ★

Did you hear about the bimbo whose boyfriend suffered from dandruff?

When she rang the chemist to ask for something to cure it, he recommended Head and Shoulders. A few days later, she rang back to say, "how do you give him shoulders?"

★ ★ ★

"Oh no!" exclaimed the dumb bloke to his mate, "I think the cops are behind us."

"Well are they flashing?" asked the driver.

"Hold on, I'll have a look. Yeah, no, yeah, no..."

★ ★ ★

279

When her two cats died, the heartbroken spinster decided to take them to the taxidermist to be stuffed.

"Certainly miss," said the taxidermist obligingly, "and do you want them mounted?"

"Oh no!" she exclaimed "Just side by side."

★ ★ ★

Three simpletons went on holiday together and ended up sharing a double bed. However it was a bit of a tight squeeze so one of them got out and tried to make himself comfortable in an easy chair. After a few minutes, he got a tap on the shoulder.

"Hey Jake, you can come back to bed, there's plenty of room now."

★ ★ ★

"Oh doctor," cried the naive young girl. "I think there's something wrong with me. My Frank and I have been trying to have a baby for six months but nothing's happened."

"Don't worry," said the kindly doctor. "I'm sure it's not too serious. If you'll just pop onto the bed and take your knickers off..."

"Oh doctor," she interrupted, "I'd rather have my husband's baby."

★ ★ ★

Two girls who'd lived their whole lives up in the mountains, were on their first visit to a big city. Everything was very strange. Round mid-day they spotted a hot dog stand and the delicious smell made them realise how hungry they were.

"I didn't know they ate dogs here," remarked one of them as they unwrapped their purchases.

"Neither did I," replied the other, looking down at her food. "What part of the dog did you get?"

★ ★ ★

Two simple hunters were out in the forest when they spotted a herd of red deer. In their haste to shoot as many as they could, one of the hunters accidentally shot his mate in the stomach. Filled with anguish, he started to drag him through the undergrowth looking for help and fortunately came across a group of walkers. He told them what had happened.

"Do you think he'll be all right?" he asked.

"I don't know," came the reply, "he'd have had a better chance if you hadn't gutted him first."

★ ★ ★

Two down-and-out robbers decided to break into a bank. They managed to by-pass the security systems and were soon inside. To their surprise, instead of one large safe, there were hundreds of smaller ones so they guessed they were in for a long stint of hard work. After ten minutes, they managed to open the first safe, only to find it contained nothing more than a bowl of semolina-type pudding. Not having eaten for some days, they wolfed it down and started on the next safe. But again it just contained this pudding which they ate. Eventually they opened all the safes, ate all the puddings but left no richer and feeling slightly nauseous. The next morning on the 9 O'clock News, local radio reported that Ireland's most famous sperm bank had been robbed during the night.

★ ★ ★

The overweight hillbilly returned to the dietician a month later to be told he'd lost a stone in weight.

"Well done," said the dietician, "and you kept strictly to my instructions, did you? Two days of eating, skip a day and just drink fluids, then eat for a further two days, skip a day, and so on..."

"Yes," replied the hillbilly, "but it was very hard. I thought I was going to burst."

"Why?"

"It was all skipping!"

★ ★ ★

Why did the dumb prisoners get caught while trying to escape?

They asked the guards to put the searchlights on so they could see where they were going.

★ ★ ★

Two simple men are sitting in a bar watching the TV. The main story on the Six O'Clock News is the suicide of a man from a 20-storey building. The camera zooms in to show him standing on the window ledge.

"I tell you what, Mick," said his mate.

"I bet you £5 he jumps."

"Okay, you're on," said Mick.

Moments later, the man jumps and hits the pavement stone dead.

"Here's your money," says Mick, getting a fiver out of his pocket.

"No, put it away," replies his mate. "I can't take your money. I saw this story on the earlier news."

"Yeah, so did I," says Mick, "but I didn't think he'd do it again."

★ ★ ★

All night the naive young Italian man had been smitten by a girl at the bar. He thought she was gorgeous but it took four stiff drinks before he had the courage to go and speak to her. After a few minutes of conversation, she leaned towards him seductively and whispered

"What I really like is a man who can deliver."

So he went out and brought her back a pizza.

★ ★ ★

"What a miserable life I've had," thought Bob sadly, as he sipped his beer at the corner of the bar. "Here I am, my 25th birthday today, and I still haven't been out with a girl. If only I wasn't so skinny, if only people would stop calling me bean pole." He ordered another half-pint and suddenly felt a tap on his shoulder. To his amazement, a woman was smiling at him and asking if she could join him. A dream come true! For the next thirty minutes, he was in seventh heaven and he was nearly fit to burst when she invited him back to her flat. When they arrived, she suggested he go into the bedroom and take all his clothes off. She would join him in a moment. He lay there shivering with anticipation when she walked in with a ten year old boy and said

"Now see here Billy, that's what you'll look like when you grow up, if you don't eat your greens."

★ ★ ★

What do you get when you cross an Irishman with a gorilla? Nothing. A gorilla is too smart to fuck an Irishman.

★ ★ ★

How can you tell an Irish firing squad?
They're the ones standing in a circle.

★ ★ ★

Posh and Becks have just returned from New York and are taking a taxi home. As is the case with taxi drivers, they have to get into conversation.

"Been anywhere nice, then, guv?" he asks.

"Yeah," replies Becks, "New York."

"Oh nice, very nice," answers the taxi driver approvingly. "Do anything special there?"

"Went to a great restaurant," says Becks.

The taxi driver continues "I lived in New York for six months, you know. Did an exchange with a New York cabbie. I probably know the restaurant. What was it called?"

Becks thinks for a moment and replies "I can't remember, give us the name of a London station."

"Euston."

"No."

"St Pancras."

"No."

"Paddington."

"No."

"Victoria."

"Yeah, that's it. Victoria," he says, turning to Posh, "what was the name of that great restaurant?"

★ ★ ★

What's a dumb man's idea of oral sex?

Walking down the street shouting "fuck you" at all the women.

★ ★ ★

Did you hear about the simple man who decided to eat outside? It rained so hard, it took him two hours to finish his soup.

★ ★ ★

The two condemned men were taken outside to be hanged. Jake got up on the platform, the rope was put round his neck but as the lever was pulled, the knot slipped and he fell into the river below. Quick as a flash he swam away and escaped. Brian was then taken up onto the platform and just as they put the rope round his neck, he said vehemently

"Now, just you be sure you don't mess up with the rope like the last one. I can't swim."

★ ★ ★

The old country folk had lived up in the hills for as far back as anyone could remember. But the day came when it was necessary to accept a few more up-to-date appliances. A new inside toilet was installed and it was decided that the old outhouse would be blown up by dynamite. The day came to raze the building to the ground and it was the two youngest sons that were given the honour of lighting the fuse. A moment later, the whole building erupted in a mighty bang and to everyone's astonishment, old Grandpa appeared staggering from the rubble. He turned to the two boys and said

"Whatever you do lads, for hell's sake, don't eat any of your grandma's friggin' bean stew."

★ ★ ★

A bloke was walking along the street when he was set upon by two muggers. He put up a terrific fight but was eventually wrestled to the ground and received a black eye, two broken ribs and a bloody nose. When the muggers searched him, they found just 20p in his pocket.

"Hey!" they exclaimed. "Why did you get yourself half killed and all for the sake of 20p?"

"I didn't want people to know I was so poor," he groaned.

★ ★ ★

A simple country lad was called up for the air force and after some instruction, he was prepared for his first parachute jump.

"After ten seconds, pull this string," he was told, "and if it doesn't work, then pull the string on the other side. When you land, we'll have a truck there to bring you back."

The lad nodded and a few minutes later, jumped out of the plane. But alas, ten seconds later the parachute failed to open. He did as he was instructed and pulled the other string but still nothing happened. The young lad muttered to himself

"Knowing my luck, the bloody truck won't be there either."

★ ★ ★

Two men had been drinking all afternoon and could barely stand up. Suddenly, one of them staggered off and disappeared for ten minutes. When he finally returned, the other said to him
"Where the fuck did you go?"
"For a piss," came the reply.
"Do us a favour, go for me now."
"Okay," so the man disappeared again and on his return said
"You prat, you didn't need to go!"

★ ★ ★

Just as the prisoner was to be marched out to the gallows, the kindly warden asked him if he'd like a shot of whisky.
"No thanks," he replied, "I've only got to have one glass and I'm all over the place."

★ ★ ★

MEET THE SERVICEMAN

A new recruit was shipped out to a faraway desert fortress to take up a twelve-month posting. After a couple of days of settling in, he was awoken one morning by the sound of great merriment. As he looked out of the window he saw the whole camp dancing around in joy.

"Quick," said his roommate, "let's get up onto the battlements and get a good view."

Puzzled, the new recruit followed the others up onto the look out stations and saw a cloud of dust moving towards them from the west.

"What's going on?" he asked.

"The goats are coming," came the reply, "and when you've been stuck here for six months without any female company, they're a very welcome sight indeed."

As the goats came into view, the men left their posts and began running towards them.

"Why are they doing that?" he asked.

"Surely there's more than enough for everyone."

"Oh yes," came the reply, "but no one wants to get stuck with an ugly one."

★ ★ ★

The survival expert was giving last minute instructions to a team of new recruits who were off to spend a couple of nights on Dartmoor.

"Just remember team, always have some flares, water, chocolate to keep up your energy, a second pair of clothes in case the first get wet, a torch and a compass... oh yes, and a pack of cards."

The new recruits quickly made notes. Then one stuck his hand up and asked

"Sir, I'm not sure how a pack of cards will help us survive."

"Well, that could possibly be the most important part of the whole knapsack," he replied. "If you get marooned, get your pack of cards out and start playing Patience. You can bet your bottom dollar that after five minutes, some nosy parker will come along and say "red five on the black six!"

★ ★ ★

The troops were behind enemy lines, holed up in the basement of an old chateau. Look-outs were placed in strategic points around the grounds and it was one of these that gave the alarm signal just before dusk on the sixth day.

"Quick, everyone below," whispered the troop leader. "Get into the cellar and stay very, very quiet."

They all hid in the basement. All as quiet as mice except for the constant sound of clink, clink, clink.

"What's that bloody noise!" exclaimed the leader. "Hobbs, see to it pronto."

A few minutes passed, the noise stopped and Hobbs returned.

"What was it?" they asked.

"Mitchell, sir, in the old toilet, wanking," replied Hobbs.

"Good man Hobbs. You stopped him then?"

"No sir. I removed the brass buttons on his cuffs."

★ ★ ★

A youth walked into the public conveniences and saw a man in a uniform, washing his hands.

"Hey, are you a sailor?"

"Yes, son," replied the man, "from the warship moored in the bay."

"Oh wow!" exclaimed the youth, his eyes shining with enthusiasm. "I've always wanted to join up."

"Here," laughed the sailor, "try my hat on for size."

Just at that moment another naval man appeared. "Are you on the warship as well?" he asked.

"Yes," he replied, "Why? do you want to suck my dick?"

"Oh no," replied the boy quickly. "I'm not a real sailor, I'm only trying on the hat."

★ ★ ★

A visiting general was inspecting the troops out on manoeuvres. As he passed a group of soldiers, disguised as trees, one of them made a sudden movement.

"Now soldier," said the General sternly, "if you move like that, you'll blow the cover of everyone."

"Sorry sir," stammered the distressed soldier. "Yesterday, I stayed stock still when two crows started to build a nest in my top branches. Today, I didn't move a muscle when a dog peed up against my trunk, but General, sir, when I heard two squirrels say let's get the two nuts and take them back to our nest, I just had to do something."

★ ★ ★

General Carruthers and his wife were hosting the summer ball. All was going well until a rather distressed woman took the General aside and complained.

"Really Maurice, your wife has all but accused me of being a lady of the night."

"Take no notice, Lady Charlotte," he blustered. "I left the army fifteen years ago and she still calls me General."

★ ★ ★

Three generals out on manoeuvres were boasting about which of their regiments showed the greatest courage.

"Now look here," said General Smythe.

"Watch this. Hey you, private, jump across that ravine."

"Yes sir," came the reply, and the private attempted to jump over the ravine but missed and plunged to his death.

"There," said the General smugly. "That's what I call courage."

"No, no, my dear man. Watch this," said the second General and he called to one of his men.

"Bates, take this message to HQ. It's urgent, so you'll have to go through the minefield."

So Bates set off, but unlucky for him, just as he was halfway across, he stood on a mine and was blown to pieces.

"Now that's what I call courage," said the second General.

"Wait, wait," protested the third General. "Just listen to this."

"Corporal Jones," he shouted. "Take that raft and make your way to the other side," he said, pointing to a fast flowing river that was only 200 yards from a steep waterfall.

"Oh bugger off General," came the reply. "You must be joking, you've been at the whisky again."

"Now gentlemen," said the third General, smiling at his two colleagues. "That's got to take the greatest courage of all."

★ ★ ★

An old desert rat was telling fellow members of the regiment's club about his solution to loneliness when he was so far from home.

"Superb idea, if I say so myself," he began. "Each time I travelled to distant lands I would take a life size picture of the latest pin up. I'd get a hole drilled in the right place and whenever I felt like letting off steam, I'd get out the picture and relieve the tension, so to speak. Kept me going for months."

Just at that moment, the old man's chauffeur arrived and one of the men who had been listening to the story commented "Your old Colonel certainly had some good ideas, didn't he?"

"Mmm," snorted the chauffeur. "I was his personal assistant on these trips and I bet the old fart didn't tell you how he always made me bend over behind the picture."

★ ★ ★

A wounded soldier was caught behind enemy lines and sent to the local internment camp. While there, his wounds became badly infected and it was decided that his leg would have to be amputated. The soldier turned to one of the guards and said "I know you've got a twenty four hour pass coming up. Would you mind sending my leg home in a parcel so that it can be buried in my own country?"

Out of sympathy, the guard agreed. However, the solider got worse and more limbs had to be amputated. One hand, another leg, and one arm were sent back to his own country in separate parcels, each time the guard had time off. Then one day, the commanding officer called in the guard and asked him what was going on. After listening to the explanation, he responded angrily "You thick prat. Don't you realise he's trying to escape."

★ ★ ★

The troops were out on manoeuvres in the Himalayas, when one of the animals carrying their supplies collapsed and died.

"You two men there," shouted the Corporal, "bury this animal immediately."

As the men dug the hole, one remarked to the other "Poor old donkey."

"That's not a donkey, that's a mule," said his mate.

Neither would agree so they asked the opinion of a third soldier.

"Trust me lads," he said, "that's an ass."

Some time later, just as they were finishing off the hole, a passing Colonel stopped to speak.

"Is that a foxhole you're digging men?" he asked.

"No, sir," replied the men saluting, "we're digging an asshole."

★　★　★

The group sergeant was showing the young recruit round the camp and was just telling him about the entertainment facilities.

"On Mondays, it's film night," he said, "and you can put in a request for anything you'd like to see."

"I don't go to the cinema," said the recruit.

"Well, on Tuesdays, it's darts night and there's always a prize for the overall winner."

"Sorry, sir, I don't play darts."

"Then on Wednesdays," continued the sergeant, impatiently, "we have a snooker tournament."

"I don't like snooker, sir," replied the recruit, shaking his head.

"Well, you'll like Thursdays, the girls from town come up for a social evening."

"No time for girls, sir," he said.

"What! Don't tell me you're gay?"

"Oh no, sir."

"Damn, you're not going to like Friday nights either, then."

★ ★ ★

The young journalist was interviewing the old fighter pilot. "I believe I'm right in saying that you used to fly across the channel many times every day, searching out enemy ships."

"That's right son," replied the man.

"And can you give me any idea what it was like?"

"It was like making love in a canoe."

"Really? How come?"

"Fucking close to water," came the reply.

★ ★ ★

MEET THE SMART ALEC

What's the difference between men and women when they fill the car up with petrol?
The men always give the hose a few shakes when they've finished.

★ ★ ★

Did you hear about the man who lost two fingers in the sawmill?
Strangely enough, he didn't notice they were missing until he waved goodbye to the foreman.

★ ★ ★

Why is pubic hair curly?
Because if it wasn't, it would blind you.

★ ★ ★

Did you hear about the poor old spinster who dreamt she got married?
When she woke up there was nothing in it.

★ ★ ★

Did you hear about the shy musician out on his first date?
He was so backward, when the girl told him she wanted to play
with his organ, he took out his harmonica.

★ ★ ★

Women's Lib is making him sleep on the wet bit.

★ ★ ★

Have you heard about the frigid woman?
Every time she opened her legs, the central heating went on.

★ ★ ★

**What's the similarity between a poultry breeder and a
prostitute?**
They both raise cocks for a living.

★ ★ ★

Ladies:
What do you call a man doing the washing up?
A start.

★ ★ ★

**What's the difference between a woman who smokes a pipe
and a woman who likes hard sex?
One likes rough shag and the other likes to shag rough.**

★ ★ ★

Did you hear about the Irish tourist officer who got sacked after
one week in the job?
His first leaflet was entitled
"Why not Bangor this weekend."

★ ★ ★

**How do you make a bull work very hard?
Give him a tight Jersey.**

★ ★ ★

What do you get when you cross a really offensive person with a
celebrity?
Dick Van go fuck yourself Dyke.

★ ★ ★

**What do you call Einstein masturbating?
A stroke of genius.**

★ ★ ★

"Have you lived in this house all your life?
"Not yet."

★ ★ ★

**"Julie," he said arrogantly, "did you know that all really
great lovers are slightly deaf?"**
"No," she replied, "I didn't."
"What?"

★ ★ ★

When do men act like gentlemen?
The time before they get to fuck their new girlfriends.

★ ★ ★

Why did the girl have her postcode tattooed on her thigh?
She hoped for some male in her box.

★ ★ ★

Why did the man put 10p in his condom?
If he couldn't come, then at least he could call.

★ ★ ★

What can the average Englishman do in four minutes?
Sup a pint, fart and make love to his wife.

★ ★ ★

She's had so many facelifts, when she smells something her forehead twitches.

★ ★ ★

Did you hear about the man who drank a bottle of spot remover by mistake?
He dropped out of sight.

★ ★ ★

He's so thin, when he drinks a tomato juice he looks like a thermometer.

★ ★ ★

Why is a male stud like a drugs' officer?
They're both crack investigators.

★ ★ ★

How does a girl avoid pregnancy?
She uses her head.

★ ★ ★

Did you hear about the man who was so bowlegged, they hung him over the door for good luck?

★ ★ ★

Why don't women have hair on their chests?
You don't get grass growing on a playground.

★ ★ ★

Why do most men never wear short-sleeved shirts?
They've got to have somewhere to wipe their noses.

★ ★ ★

Did you hear about the man whose mistress kept demanding such expensive presents?
He ended up having to marry her for his money.

★ ★ ★

What did the dumb woman do when she read a notice in the public conveniences saying
"Don't put anything down the toilet but toilet paper?"
She shat on the floor.

★ ★ ★

Have you heard about the new clockwork doll?
It's called the 'dole doll'. When you wind it up, it doesn't work.

★ ★ ★

Having feasted magnificently on a stray bull, the lion roared with satisfaction. However, the sound carried to a group of hunters who tracked him down and shot him.
So please beware: If you're full of bull, keep your mouth shut.

★ ★ ★

Why do so many mothers cry at weddings?
It's because the daughters usually marry someone like their fathers.

★ ★ ★

The man had got such a huge spare tyre, he used to leave tread marks on his girlfriend.

★ ★ ★

What's the definition of sex?
One damp thing after another.

★ ★ ★

Have you noticed that people who have irritating coughs never go to the doctor's... they go to the theatre, the cinema, the concert...

★ ★ ★

What's the difference between hard and dark?
It stays dark all night long.

★ ★ ★

Girls, what can you do to be sure you get something hard between your legs?
Buy a motorbike.

★ ★ ★

Scrawled on a toilet wall:
Always aim high... then you won't splash your shoes.

★ ★ ★

There had been such heavy snow overnight that the poor little bird was unable to find adequate shelter and fell to the ground in a dead faint. As time passed, a cow ambled along and dropped a cow pat on top of it. The dung was so warm, the little bird began to thaw out and was so overjoyed at his surprise rescue that he sang at the top of his voice. Unfortunately for him, a mean old cat came along, heard the singing, discovered the little bird and ate it.
So, people beware.
Not everyone who drops shit on you is an enemy and not everyone who gets you out of shit is a friend. Even more importantly, when you find you're in deep shit, keep your mouth shut.

★ ★ ★

Did you hear the sad story about the karate champion who joined the air force?
On the first day, he saluted his commanding officer a little too enthusiastically, and killed himself.

★ ★ ★

Did you hear about the man who was so lazy, he eventually had to go to hospital to have his chair surgically removed from his arse!

* * *

Fellahs, what's the definition of a goblin teas made?
A maid who comes into your bedroom first thing in the morning with a tray of cups and saucers and a teapot, then pulls out your penis and gives you a blow job!

* * *

The woman was so fat that one day when she hung her bloomers out to dry, a family of gypsies moved in.

* * *

Have you heard about the revolutionary birthday cake made out of beans?
It blows out its own candles!

* * *

**What's the similarity between men and public conveniences?
All the good ones are engaged and the only ones left are full of shit.**

* * *

Why do the female black widow spiders kill the males after mating?
To stop the snoring before it starts.

★ ★ ★

What's the difference between a blonde and a mosquito?
A mosquito stops sucking when you slap it.

★ ★ ★

What's the definition of obscenity?
Anything that gives the judge an erection.

★ ★ ★

Have you ever wondered why kamikaze pilots wore helmets?

★ ★ ★

How do you know if a girl is too fat to fuck?
When you pull her knickers down, her arse is still in them.

★ ★ ★

What's the best thing about a blow job?
A few minutes peace and quiet.

★ ★ ★

"No, no, no," exclaimed the female centipede, crossing her legs, "a thousand times no."

★ ★ ★

He must be the unluckiest ex-husband alive!
He missed two maintenance payments on the trot, and she repossessed him.

★ ★ ★

What is virgin wool?
A sheep the farmer hasn't caught yet.

★ ★ ★

"How do you prepare your turkey?" asked the trainee chef.
"Very honestly," came the reply. "We just come right out and tell them they're for the chop."

★ ★ ★

How do you know when your first date is going to be really successful?
When you ask your girl to dance and she gets up on the table.

★ ★ ★

How did Captain Hook die
Jock itch.

★ ★ ★

Why did the girl complain about oral sex?
She thought it was a lousy view.

★ ★ ★

Why is a blonde like an oven?
They're both easy to heat up before sticking the meat in.

★ ★ ★

Did you hear about the prisoner found unconscious in his cell?
He'd tried to hang himself with a rubber band.

★ ★ ★

What have you got if you have pieces of glass in a condom?
An organ grinder.

★ ★ ★

What's the similarity between masturbation and a game
of solitaire?
If you've a good hand, you don't need partners.

★ ★ ★

What's the difference between a woman of 40 years and a man of 40 years?
The woman thinks of having children, the man thinks about dating them.

★ ★ ★

Why are women and rocks alike?
You skip the flat ones.

★ ★ ★

Did you hear about the man who swallowed a Viagra tablet too slowly?
He got a stiff neck.

★ ★ ★

What is making love?
It's something a woman does while a man is fucking her.

★ ★ ★

Why is Adam known as the first accountant?
He turned a leaf and made an entry.

★ ★ ★

You know you're getting old when you have a party and the neighbours don't complain.

★ ★ ★

What do you call a man who wants sex on the second date? Slow.

★ ★ ★

Why did the rubber fly across the room?
It got pissed off.

★ ★ ★

How do we know God is a man?
Because if God were a woman, sperm would taste like chocolate.

★ ★ ★

Why do men have a hole in their penis?
So their brains can get some oxygen now and again.

★ ★ ★

MEET THE SPORTSMAN

Why do men enjoy fishing so much?
It's the only time people will say to them
"Cor! that's a big one."

★ ★ ★

A man has just played a gruelling five-set tennis match and in a rush to have a drink in the bar afterwards, he puts the tennis balls in the pockets of his trousers.
As he's sipping his pint, he notices a girl looking strangely at the bulges in his trousers.
"Oh, tennis balls," he says in embarrassment.
"Really?" she replies. "That must be painful. I had tennis elbow once."

★ ★ ★

Two women watching Rugby League.
"Great tackle," called out one.
"Nice bum, too," added the other.

★ ★ ★

Why did the battered wife decide to live with the English cricket team?
They don't beat anybody.

★ ★ ★

"Did you notice the football team ogling that girl as she walked by?" the wife asked her husband.
"What football team," came the reply.

★ ★ ★

Two men were down in Hell, stoking the fire the way they had done it for the past twenty years. Then one day, to their astonishment, it began to snow. And the snow got heavier and heavier till eventually the fire went out and the icy wind blew.
"Bloody hell," said one, "what's going on?"
"It looks as if England have won the Ashes," replied the other.

★ ★ ★

It had been a long and gruelling wrestling match. The advantage swung from one contestant to the other with no one getting the upper hand. Then, out of the blue, the champion managed to get his opponent into his favourite hold and for the crowd, it looked as if the whole match was over.

But suddenly, to everyone's amazement, there came a mighty roar and the champion went flying through the air, lay on his back stunned, and was counted out. After the match, the winning trainer came over to his man and said, "I can't believe Ken, I thought it was all over when he got you in that hold."

"So did I," agreed the man, "but when I opened my eyes and saw this pair of balls in front of my face, I bit them as hard as I could and do you know, it's amazing how much strength you have when you bite your own balls!"

★ ★ ★

One sunny Sunday morning, a couple of women were teeing off on the ninth fairway when one of them hooked wildly and the ball soared through the air straight to a group of golfers on the next hole.

To their dismay, they heard a scream and as they ran to apologise, they found a man rolling around in agony on the ground.

"Oh my goodness," gasped the woman looking down on the curled up figure of the man, groaning loudly, his hands clasped between his legs.

"I'm sure I can help you," she said. "I'm a masseuse and I can relieve the pain."

Ignoring his protests, she knelt on the ground undid his

trousers and began to gently massage him. After a few minutes she said, "There, how does that feel?"

"Fine," he replied with a satisfied look on his face, "but my thumb still hurts terribly."

★ ★ ★

The local tennis club was having its annual competition and Steve had just beaten Malcolm, a notoriously bad loser. In the bar afterwards, Malcolm passed Steve and running his hand over Steve's bald head, remarked "My goodness, your head feels just like my wife's backside."

Quick as a flash Steve stroked his head and replied "Well I never, it does, doesn't it?"

★ ★ ★

"I say James, did you take my advice and get those new bifocals?"

"Yes, thanks Martin, I did, and it improved my golf dramatically as you said it would. When I looked down I saw two balls, a big one and a little one, and when I looked at the green, I saw a big hole and a little hole. So I just hit the small ball into the big hole and hey presto!"

"So why aren't you wearing them now?"

"Bit of a faux pas," replied James. "Wet my trousers, don't you know. After the game I went to the toilet, looked down

and saw one small 'fellow' and one large. Well I knew the big
one couldn't be mine, so I put it away again."

★ ★ ★

A husband was being asked by the coroner's court the
circumstances surrounding his wife's death.

"It was a dreadful accident," he said. "I was teeing off at the
seventh hole, when I hooked it badly and it hit my wife on the
head. She died later."

"Yes," agreed the coroner, "that seems to explain the injuries,
but could you please tell me why she had a golf ball stuck up
her arse?"

"Well, the first shot had been so bad, I decided to take it again."

★ ★ ★

Two blokes were in the Clubhouse having drinks. One turned
to the other and said "I say, did you hear about poor old
Malcolm. Pressure got to him, you know. Went berserk
yesterday and beat his wife to death with a golf club."

"Poor show," replied Gerald, "but just for the record, how
many strokes?"

★ ★ ★

Two football fans were down at the front of the crowd when some yobbo towards the back started to throw beer cans. One of the fans got very agitated and couldn't concentrate on the game properly.

"Don't worry," said his mate. "It's like the war, if it's got your name on it..."

"That's the trouble," interrupted the other. "My name's Fosters."

★ ★ ★

A horse was walking by the village green when he spotted a game of cricket in progress. He went over to the Captain and asked "Any chance of a game?"

The Captain looked dumbfounded when he heard the horse talk but it so happened that one of his team had just retired injured so he agreed to put him in at number 7. The horse was sensational. He hit a four or a six off every ball in the over and the crowd were going wild. However, when the bowler changed ends, batsman 6 hit a single.

"Run," he shouted to the horse, "run, quick." But the horse didn't move an inch and the batsman was run out.

"Why didn't you run?" he demanded, as he left the field.

"Listen," said the horse angrily. "If I could run I'd be at the racecourse now, not stuck in some bloody village cricket team."

★ ★ ★

"It's no good Bernard, I can't play anymore, it's the old stomach, not so good," said Lewis as the two friends walked onto the ninth fairway.

"That's a shame," replied Bernard. "Are you sure?"

"Very. To tell you the truth, I farted at the last hole."

"Well that's no big deal."

"No, but you see, the trouble is, I followed through."

★ ★ ★

MEET THE TRAVELLER

A young man finds himself stranded on the moor after his car breaks down. He sets off for help and comes across a house standing alone. It's now midnight and very cold. The owner of the house, a Chinaman, agrees to let the traveller stay overnight but he warns him sternly that his daughter is also in the house and he must not have any contact with her. Otherwise he will have to suffer three horrible tortures. The man agrees and settles down to sleep. But suddenly he hears this beautiful singing and has to get up to investigate. He opens the door to the adjoining room and there is the most gorgeous girl he's ever seen, sitting up in bed singing as she brushes her long black silky hair. The young man is overcome with passion and before the night is much older, he has joined her in her bed. At dawn, he returns to his own room and falls into a deep satisfying sleep. However, when he wakes a couple of hours later, he finds a big stone on his chest and next to it a note which says

"This is Torture 1."

"Bollocks," he thinks to himself, and picking up the huge stone, he staggers to the window and throws it out. But as he watches it hurtling to the ground, he sees another note pinned to the window, "Torture 2, stone tied to left testicle."

Acting quickly, he jumps out of the window, thinking it would be better to break a few bones than suffer the alternative. But as he leaps out he sees the third and final note staring up at him from the ground. "Torture 3 – right testicle tied to bedroom door."

★ ★ ★

The young couple had been out on their first date and as they drove home, passions were running high. Then disaster struck. Just as they got to the top of a steep hill, the engine stalled and they came to a sudden halt. Steve jumped out and crawled underneath the car to see what was wrong and a few minutes later, Sandra joined him. As they lay there, side by side, lust took over and soon they were in the throes of unbridled passion.

"It's all right," he whispered, "no one can see us under here." But a few minutes later, a big pair of boots came into view and as Steve looked up he saw a policeman, looking down.

"Now what's going on here?" he demanded.

"Well... er... the car stalled," stammered Steve, trying to pull his clothes together. "And I was just trying to find out what caused it."

"Well, if I was you, I'd take a look at the brakes at the same time, your car's 100 yards further down the road."

★ ★ ★

On another occasion when the car stalled on a hill the man turned to his girlfriend and asked

"Shall we get out and push it up?"

"Yeah," she replied, "but will it be all right to leave the car here?"

★ ★ ★

Colin liked to boast, he couldn't help it. Wherever he went, whatever he did – it was always better than anyone else. His latest hobby was big game hunting and before he left for Africa he boasted he would bring back a big gorilla. Three days into his safari, he disappeared into the jungle and spotted a gorilla disappearing into the undergrowth. He took aim and fired. But when he went to retrieve his prize, there was no sign of the animal. Suddenly, he felt a tap on the shoulder and looking round, the gorilla was standing behind him.

"Right," he roared. "You disturbed my afternoon stroll. For that, you're going to give me a blow job."

Terrified, the man did as he was told and returned to camp, thankful he'd survived. But now he was even more determined to shoot the gorilla. So armed with an even deadlier gun, he returned to the same spot the next day. Alas, he fired but missed again. So once more he administered to the animal's wishes before being sent on his way.

"Damned, damned, damned," he cursed. "I'll get that bloody animal if it kills me. It'll be the best trophy in the Club house when I get home."

Early the next day, he set out stealthily and got to the clearing in good time. He lifted the gun to his shoulder to check the telescopic sight when he heard a mighty roar behind him.

"Okay, get down on your knees," snarled the gorilla and give me another blow job."
The man complied and just as he finished, the gorilla commented "You know, sometimes I think the hunting is just an excuse."

★ ★ ★

Two teachers are returning home from a two-day course when their car breaks down and they are forced to spend the night at an hotel. Unfortunately, all the single rooms are taken so they have to share a double. The woman gets ready for bed changing in the bathroom, then the man does the same. Later, as they both lay there, the woman realises she's got the hots for her colleague but is too shy to do anything about it. Instead, she makes idle conversation.

"Listen Derek, it sounds as if we have a dripping tap."

Derek turns to her and replies

"I have an idea Doreen," he says. "How about just for tonight we pretend we're man and wife."

"Oh yes," she says excitedly, "that's wonderful. I'd love to."

"Good," he says, angrily, "then go and turn the bloody thing off yourself."

★ ★ ★

A man was travelling through the countryside when his car suddenly made a spluttering noise and came to a halt.

"Oh bugger," he cursed, as he lifted the bonnet to find out what was wrong. "It'll be dirty spark plugs," said a voice behind him, and looking round in surprise, he realised it was a horse speaking to him from a nearby field. He was still standing there open-mouthed in astonishment when a mechanic drew up beside him.

"Anything I can do?" he called.

"Oh yes, yes," replied the man. "My car has stalled. But you'll think I'm mad if I tell you that the horse in that field over there, told me it was the spark plugs."

"Oh don't listen to him," replied the mechanic dismissively. "He's never bloody right."

★ ★ ★

Due to fog at Heathrow, the 4.15 flight to Washington was cancelled and the passengers queued up to be reallocated seats on other services. As they waited patiently for it to be sorted, a big red-faced man barged his way through to the front of the queue.

"I demand immediate attention," he bellowed. "I have to be on the next flight to Washington and I insist on first class."

The flight official looked at him sympathetically and replied "I understand your frustration sir. But we will sort this problem out as quickly as possible, so if you'd like to get back into line..."

"Why! How dare you fob me off. Do you know who I am?" he shouted.

The girl smiled at him and turned on the public address system.

"Attention all passengers. I have a gentleman here at gate 7 who doesn't know who he is. If anyone can help, please contact us as soon as possible. Thank you."

★ ★ ★

When the man entered the sleeper compartment, the girl in the lower bunk had already gone to sleep. Quietly, he climbed up into the top bunk, switched off the light but in doing so, his toupee slipped off and landed below.

"Damn!" he cursed under his breath as he blindly felt around for his toupee. Suddenly, he put his hand on some hair and at that moment the girl cried out in her sleep.

"That's it. Good. Oh yes, please." He continued to feel around when the girl spoke again

"More, more, it's yours, it's yours."

The man took his hand away quickly.

"I'm so sorry miss," he said, "you're quite mistaken. I part mine down the side."

★ ★ ★

A young couple went on a safari to Africa, accompanied by the woman's mother. On the second day, they got separated from their party and found themselves in a remote part of the jungle. Suddenly, a lion jumped out of the undergrowth and stood growling ferociously in front of the mother-in-law.

"Quick George," screamed the wife, "do something."

"Not bloody likely," he replied, "the lion got himself into this mess, now he can get himself out."

★ ★ ★

Lost in the dark wild moors of Dartmoor, the young man finally spotted a light in the distance. As he got nearer he saw a small cottage nestling in the valley and he walked hopefully up to the door.

"I'm sorry to bother you," he said, as the door was opened by an old man, "my car has broken down and I'm afraid I'm completely lost."

"Come in son," said the old man kindly, "it's not a night to be out on the moors."

The man was ushered inside where he met the old wife and their daughter Ida, sitting round a blazing fire. They gave him supper and then suggested he could bed down on the sofa for the night. The man gratefully accepted. By 2 o'clock in the morning, the storm had worsened and the old man turned to his wife and said

"I think I'll just go down and make sure our guest is all right." He hobbled down the stairs and whispered

"Are you warm enough? Do you want any more blankets?"

"No thanks," came the reply. "I'm fine."

"Are you sure you wouldn't like a hot water bottle?"

"No, really, it's okay."

"Well what about our eiderdown?"

"Good gracious!" exclaimed the man. "At this rate, I'll never get any sleep. She's been down three times already."

★ ★ ★

A rather snooty lady was travelling to Ascot when her car broke down. While she was waiting for it to be mended, she went into a nearby transport cafe and ordered breakfast.

"Young man, I'll have the all-day breakfast please. Don't overcook the egg, don't burn the toast and don't, whatever you do, give me a sausage. Ugh, the sight of a sausage makes the short curly hairs on the back of my head stand on end."

"Well, what a coincidence," replied the mischievous waiter, one sight of short curly hairs makes my sausage stand on end!"

★ ★ ★

A man is travelling home late from work when he falls asleep and misses his stop. He wakes up to find himself fifty miles from home, no more trains running and not enough money to get a taxi. However, he sees a taxi waiting by itself in the station forecourt and hopes the driver will be sympathetic to his story. But no. The taxi driver won't take him on trust, so the poor man has to hitch-hike, getting home at three in the morning. The man is out for revenge. A few days later he travels to the station again and is relieved to see four taxis waiting for fares, one of which is the bastard from the other night. Leaving this man to last, he goes up to the other three in turn and tells them he hasn't got enough money for the fare but if they take him home, he'll give them a blow job. All three tell him to piss off. Then he goes up to the fourth taxi, tells him the destination, gets in and off they go. Satisfied at his success, he passes the other cabbies, grins at them through the window and gives the thumbs up sign.

★ ★ ★

"Ladies and gentlemen," announced the airline pilot, "due to a loss of power in one of our four engines, we will now land in San Francisco an hour late. Our apologies for any inconvenience caused."
Five minutes later, he made another announcement.
"A second engine has failed but please be assured that the plane can fly on the two remaining engines. It will just mean a further delay of another thirty minutes."
Then later still, he made a third announcement.
"Due to the failure of a third engine, we will now be landing at San Francisco three hours later than scheduled."
At this point, one of the passengers exclaimed loudly
"Let's hope we don't lose the fourth engine, otherwise we'll be up here all bloody night."

★ ★ ★

The train driver called over his deputy and said
"Charlie, can you get me some cotton wool for my ears."

"What's up, Bert, are your ears hurting?"
"Not yet, but they will do when all the screaming starts, after I tell the passengers our brakes have failed."

★ ★ ★

A good time girl misses the last bus home so is forced to take a taxi. When they arrive at her door the cabbie asks for the fare of £4.50.

"I'm sorry," she says, "I ain't got any money but I could make it up to you in another way." With that, she lifts her skirt and drops her knickers. "Will that do?" she says sexily.

"Have you got anything smaller?" he replies.

★ ★ ★

The couple and their son had set up camp and the boy had wandered off to play. A few minutes later he returned with the top half of a bikini in his hand.

"Now son," said the dad thoughtfully, "just show me exactly where you found this."

★ ★ ★

"Jack, what happened?" gasped his friend on seeing him in the intensive care unit of the local hospital. "I thought you were touring in South America."

"I was," replied Jack weakly, "but it all went horribly wrong. Three weeks into the tour, our band played in this remote village and we went down such a storm that the Chief ordered all our instruments to be filled with fabulous jewels. Unfortunately, I was playing the flute at the time, so I didn't do quite so well out of it."

Jack stopped while the nurse mopped his fevered brow and then continued.

"Anyway, later we found ourselves in another out of the way village and this time the Chief hated our music so much, he order all the instruments to be shoved up our backsides."

"Wow!" exclaimed his friend, "it's a good thing you played the flute."

"But that's just the trouble," said Jack, sadly. "This time I was playing the tuba – you can't get much bigger than that."

★ ★ ★

A tourist staggers out of the bar after ten pints of beer and strays onto the nudist beach where he is confronted by a naked woman. After looking at her for a few moments, he remarks hazily

"My wife's got an outfit just like yours."

★ ★ ★

There's been a severe shortage of food in the jungle, so when a missionary appears, two cannibals start to fight over who will take the prize. Eventually, too weak to argue, they decide to share him - one starting at the top, the other at his feet, until they meet up in the middle. After eating for some minutes, one cannibal turns to the other and says, "How's it going?"

"Oh great," replies the other. "I'm having a ball."

"Oh no!" exclaims the first, "just slow down a bit, you're eating too fast."

* * *

A truck driver walked into a transport café and looked at the menu which read

"Leg of pork, bacon, black pudding, pigs trotters and pork sausage."

He ordered his meal and also asked for a glass of water.

"Certainly sir," replied the owner, "it'll be water from the bore."

"Bloody hell, you sure don't waste any of that pig!" he exclaimed.

* * *

An upper class lady walked into a vacant lift and as the doors closed, she was unable to stop herself from letting out a fart. Quickly, she took some freshener out of her bag and sprayed it around the area in case anyone else should enter.

As they got to the 10th floor, a man stepped in and sniffed the air.

"Is there anything wrong?" she asked sweetly.

"Bloody odd smell in here," he replied. "It's almost as if someone's shit in a lavender bush."

★ ★ ★

Two rival football supporters travelled home from the match in the same railway compartment. As Tony got up to go to the buffet car, he asked the other if he could get him anything. "Thanks mate," replied the man. "A glass of lager please." When Tony had gone, the rival fan gobbed in Tony's football cap which was lying on the seat. Then Tony returned and handed over the glass of lager, which he drank down greedily. At last it was Tony's stop and as he got up to leave, he put his cap on and immediately realised what had happened.
"You know mate," he said looking at the smirk on the other's face, "we've gotta stop doing all this – gobbing in caps and peeing in lager."

★ ★ ★

In a small, crowded railway carriage, an old man got out his pipe and as he lit the tobacco, clouds of smoke filled the air. An old woman turned to him in disgust and remarked "I was married to my Alfred for 52 years and not once did he put a pipe in his mouth."

Unaffected by her anger, he replied "Well Missus, I'm 65 and in all my years I've never put it anywhere else."

★ ★ ★

The Euro Express had just entered the tunnel when all the lights failed. In one of the front carriages sat an old woman, a young model, a policeman and an old lag. As they were plunged into darkness, they heard the sound of a loud kiss, followed by a sharp smack. Moments later, the lights came on and each one sat there as if nothing had happened. The old woman looked at the young model and thought:

"Good for her, how dare that copper think he can get away with such awful behaviour."

The young model thought

"Ugh, fancy that horrible looking bloke, kissing the old woman."

The policeman thought angrily

"I didn't do anything so why should I get my face slapped, and the old lag sat there contentedly thinking

"Fooled 'em all. It's not often the opportunity arises where I can kiss the air, smack a policeman and get away with it."

★ ★ ★

The woman looked with disgust at the slovenly bloke sitting opposite her in the railway carriage. His tie was askew, his clothes rumpled and he had a huge beer gut.

"You're a disgrace," she said, addressing him. "If that stomach was on a woman, she'd be pregnant."

The man smiled smugly and replied "It was...and she is."

★ ★ ★

A wealthy man was travelling through Egypt by camel but had been having a lot of trouble finding a top class animal to suit his needs. Eventually, he was advised to visit the best camel breeder in the district, Ali Bari, who would have just what he wanted.

"Good day, Ali Bari," he said. "The next stage of my trip is going to last four weeks so I need an animal that won't let me down. I don't care how much I pay."

"Very well," replied the dealer, and he took him to see a magnificent camel in his courtyard.

"This camel will get you there quite safely. Just remember to give him plenty of water before setting out."

So the wealthy man followed instructions and then travelled into the desert. But alas, after two weeks the camel dropped down dead. Fortunately, the man was rescued and was able to finish his journey soon after.

It wasn't until a year later that the man found himself back in the town when he had bought the camel from Ali Bari. He accosted the dealer saying "How dare you sell me such a poor animal. It only lasted two weeks before dropping dead. You swindled me."

The dealer protested.

"Did you give it plenty of water."

"Of course I did."

"And did you give him the two-brick treatment?"

"The two-brick treatment? What's that?"

Ali Bari replied "When you think he's just about to stop

drinking, you bang his balls between two bricks as hard as possible and he sucks in enough water to last another two weeks."

★ ★ ★

Two men were travelling in the same carriage of an old rickety rural train which did not have toilet facilities. Suddenly, one of the men said to his companion "I'm sorry, I find myself in the embarrassing position of needing the toilet very urgently. Would you mind if I just went on this piece of newspaper?"
The other gave his permission, the act was performed and the paper then thrown out of the window.
Meanwhile, the travelling companion, unable to stomach the noxious smell had lit a cigarette.
"I say," said the first man, sitting back down, "this is a non-smoking carriage, you know."

★ ★ ★

Jack, his wife and seven children were waiting for the number 27 bus. Also at the bus stop was a blind man. After twenty minutes, the bus finally arrived but it was almost full. "Only room for eight more," called out to the conductor. Immediately Jack rounded up his family and put them on the bus, taking no notice of the blind man's wishes.
"Me and the blind man will walk," he said to his wife. "I'll see you later."

The bus moved off and the two men began walking down the street accompanied by the tap, tap, tap of the white stick. After a while Jack complained.

"That bloody tap, tap, tap of the stick is getting right up my nose," he said nastily. "Can't you put a rubber on the end of it?"

"You're a right one to complain," retorted the blind man. "If you'd put a rubber on the end of your stick, we'd both be on the bus now instead of walking."

★ ★ ★

MEET THE WIFE

"Now Suzanne," said the wife to the new housemaid. "I shall be out tonight at Lady Cynthia's so you'll only be serving dinner to my husband. I hope you'll be able to cope if anything unexpected comes up?"

"Oh yes madam," she replied. "I've got a packet of condoms."

★ ★ ★

She said bitterly
"When all that is stiff is his socks, take the money and run."

★ ★ ★

A Rolls Royce pulls up outside the posh Beverley Hills hotel and the doorman walks down to greet the new guests. There are only two occupants in the car. The President of the country's leading bank and his ambitious wife Julia. She gasps when she sees the doorman then smiles and greets him warmly.

"Oh Tom, I can't believe it's you," she says, "how wonderful."

They chat for a few minutes and then she and her husband disappear inside. As they take the lift up to their penthouse suite, he asks her about the doorman.

"Oh Tommy was an old boyfriend of mine, many years ago. In fact, at one time we were engaged," she says.

"I bet you're glad you didn't marry him though," he says.

"Why do you say that?" she asks.

"Well, because I'm the President of a National Bank and he's just a lowly doorman."

His wife looks at him for a few moments and then replies coldly "What you're forgetting Gerald, is that if I had married Tommy, he would be President now."

★ ★ ★

The woman went to the beauty parlour and after her treatment, said to the beautician

"Do you think my husband will think I'm beautiful?"

"I should think so. He still drinks a lot, doesn't he?"

★ ★ ★

The husband came down to breakfast, holding his head in his hands and moaning.

"So Gerald," said his wife, "have you ever been told you're the most handsome man in town?"

"No dear."

"And have you ever been told you're the best dancer in town?"

"No dear."

"So has anyone ever told you, you're irresistible to women?"

"Certainly not dear."

"Then pray, where did you get all those silly ideas at the party last night?"

* * *

"Is that the obituary section of the Clarion?" asked the woman.

"Yes, madam, can I help you?"

"I'd like to put a notice in, reporting the death of my husband from gunshot wounds."

"Good gracious, when did it happen?"

"Just as soon as I find the cheating bugger."

* * *

"Hello Joan. You look happy today, what's going on?"

"Oh Maisie, I am," she replied. "Last night my husband brought home a big tube of KY jelly. He said it would please me greatly. And it did. When he went to the bathroom I smeared it all over the bedroom door and the silly bugger couldn't get back in!"

* * *

"You're a fool to yourself Ethel," said her neighbour scornfully. "That husband of yours has you running around in circles."

"Oh don't say that," replied Ethel with spirit. "He helps with the housework, you know. He sits in front of the television and gathers dust."

* * *

341

Said the disillusioned woman
"The only time my husband wakes up stiff is when he's been down the gym the night before."

★ ★ ★

The old couple had just finished lunch when the wife remarked
"You know James, we're not getting any younger, we've got to accept that it won't be too long before one of us passes on."
"Oh come on Ruby," he replied, "don't let's talk about such things."
"Well okay, but I just want you to know I think I'll go to Eastbourne when that happens."

★ ★ ★

The old woman turned sadly to her friend and said
"The spark's gone out of our marriage Flo. These days, when we're in bed, I bring out the animal in Alfred. He runs to the door, scratching and whining to get out. Oh dear."

★ ★ ★

An old couple had been married for thirty years, and in all that time no one could remember when he didn't chew tobacco. He was always seen with heavily stained teeth and black gunge dribbling out of his mouth. Now the thing that

puzzled their neighbours was how his wife could have stayed with him so long. In her younger days, she had been very attractive and even now, she could turn a head or two. Two days before the couple's wedding anniversary, her friend finally plucked up the courage to ask

"How could you have stayed with him so long. That awful black, filthy stuff forever dribbling from his mouth?"

"Well I have thought of leaving him on many occasions," she said, "but I couldn't bear to kiss him goodbye."

★ ★ ★

After an hour of playing bridge and getting beaten every time, the husband excused himself to go to the bathroom. As he left the room, the wife turned to her hosts and remarked scornfully,

"This'll be the first time I've known what's in his hand all night."

★ ★ ★

A woman went to the doctor's complaining that her sex life was very unsatisfactory.

"My old man says I'm frigid," she explained.

"Don't upset yourself," replied the doctor kindly. "I think I have the answer. Just take one of these pills an hour before lovemaking and you'll appreciate the difference."

So an hour before her husband was due home, the woman took the pill and as the time drew near her whole body became electric. She couldn't wait for him to walk through the door.

Unfortunately, he went straight to the pub after work and the magic moment was missed. When she went back to the doctor's, he asked her how it had gone and she explained the dreadful disappointment she'd felt and how the lack of fulfilment had made her ill.

"Mmm," mused the doctor, "it's a shame there wasn't another man to take his place."

"Another man!" she exclaimed. "I don't need pills for other men!"

★ ★ ★

A worried man went to the doctor's and asked him to come and visit his wife who was ill in bed with a bad chest infection.

"Just one thing in confidence, doctor," he said. "My wife never wears any knickers. I hate it. I beg her to change but she just won't listen to me. I wonder if you could somehow link her illness to her lack of underwear. Maybe it will convince her."

The doctor agreed and accompanied the man home. He examined the wife's throat and her chest very thoroughly.

"I'm afraid it's a touch of bronchitis," he told her. "I'll write out a prescription for you but I would also strongly recommend that you wear some knickers. It won't help your illness.

She looked at him quizzically.

"Are you trying to tell me that just by looking down my throat you could see I wasn't wearing any knickers?"

"Well...er...yes" he answered.

"In that case," she said nastily, "would you like to look up my bum and tell me if my hat's on straight."

★ ★ ★

When it was discovered that her husband had a tapeworm, the old country wife administered to his needs. Each morning she would mix up a potion of fresh herbs, carrots from the garden and freshly baked bread. Then she would shove it up his arse and follow it with a jam doughnut. This happened every day for two weeks until on the fifteenth morning, she put the potion up as usual but left out the jam doughnut.
"I don't understand," complained her husband. "After two weeks, I don't seem to be any better."
"Sssh," she whispered as they waited expectantly. All of a sudden the tapeworm poked his head out of the man's bum and said, "Hey, where's the doughnut?"
Wham! They got it with one blow.

★ ★ ★

The couple had been married for seven years and their life together had lost it's sparkle. Sex was a disaster.
"There doesn't seem to be any passion left," said her husband one day. "Maybe we should part company."
Now that filled the wife with dread because she didn't want to lose all the comforts of her married life. It would mean she'd have to find a job!

That night she was determined to show him what he would miss. She dressed in her sexiest negligee and actively started to move a bit during their lovemaking. Her husband was astonished, but delighted. The only strange thing was that every 30 minutes, she would excuse herself and disappear into the bathroom, then return and continue more passionately than before. Although the husband didn't want to spoil the moment, he got so curious he eventually had to find out what was going on. The next time she went into the bathroom, he sneaked in after her and to his amazement, she was standing in front of the mirror saying over and over again, "He's not my husband...he's not my husband...he's not my husband."

★ ★ ★

Fed up with his wife's excuse of always having a headache, the husband came up with a foolproof plan. The next time they went to bed she said, as usual, "not tonight, darling, I've got a headache."
"Really?" he replied. "Well it's a good thing I've dusted my dick in paracetamol then."

★ ★ ★

A man looked at his wife and asked delicately, "Darling, it was a great party last night...er...um, it was you I made love to in the garden, wasn't it?"

She threw him a contemptuous look and replied "I don't know, what time would that be?"

* * *

A journalist interviewed a local woman when he heard she'd had four children, all born three years apart on May 20th. "That's astonishing," he remarked, "and what does your husband do for a living?"
"Oh, he's a precision grinder," came the reply.

* * *

MEET THE WORKMATES

Did you hear about the promising young actress who had to perform live sex on stage?
By the end of the performance, there wasn't a dry handkerchief in the house.

★ ★ ★

An ageing, out of work actor, received a phone call from his agent telling him to be in Leeds the following Friday for a part in the Christmas panto. The actor was thrilled. At last, he would be treading the boards once again! However, his joy turned to despair when he realised he didn't have enough money to travel to Leeds. Then he had an idea. Early next morning he went down to the canal and engaged a bargee in conversation.

"Excuse me, bargee," he said. "I am to appear in Pantomime at Leeds Theatre next Friday and I wondered if anyone was going my way?"

"As it happens, I am," replied the bargee. I set off at six o'clock in the morning, we'll make it by Thursday as long as we get through the locks without a mishap. True to his word, the bargee set off at six the next morning with the ageing actor on board. As the first lock came into view, the lock keeper shouted down

"Hello there, what are you carrying?"

"I'm carrying 10 ton of pig shite and the actor Cyril Carstairs," replied the bargee.

At the second lock, the lock keeper asked the same question and again he got the same reply.

"I'm carrying 10 ton of pig shite and the actor Cyril Carstairs."

So the journey continued until they came to the outskirts of Leeds and the final, 22nd lock. As they approached, the actor tapped the bargee on the shoulder and said

"Excuse me, bargee, we're coming to the final lock, would it be possible just this once, for me to have top billing?"

★ ★ ★

A man walked into the business centre and said

"I would like to send some information to my girl friend in Leeds."

"Fax?" enquired the man.

"Too bloody right," he replied "like a rampant tart."

★ ★ ★

"Oooh George," cooed the girl, "you are naughty, what will your boss at British Rail think if he saw your crumpled uniform."

"Forget about that," panted George, "come on girl, get your knickers off."

"But George, we don't have any condoms."
"Not to worry, at British Rail we always pull out on time."

★ ★ ★

The local journalist had been sent to interview a woman who had eleven kids. They were all boys and she was hoping to start up her own football team.

"So Mrs Haverlot, this is your eldest son. What's his name?"

"Bobby," she said. "After Bobby Charlton."

The journalist scribbled in his notebook.

"And this lad here, what's his name?"

"Bobby," she replied.

He looked puzzled, but continued. "What about this one?"

"Bobby," she replied.

The journalist laughed. "You'll be telling me next that they're all called Bobby."

"That's right," she said.

"But how do they know who you want when you call one of them."

"Oh that's no problem," she said, "they've all got different surnames."

★ ★ ★

The ambitious P.A. went out for dinner with her boss and when the bill arrived she said

"I must insist that we go Dutch. I suggest you pay for dinner and the rest of the evening will be on me."

★ ★ ★

A young man went back to the department store to change the underpants he had bought the day before. Unfortunately, the male shop assistant was at lunch so he had to take them to a young girl and felt rather embarrassed when she asked what was wrong with them.

Suddenly, he had an idea.

"Have you been to the Tower of London?" he asked.

"Yes," she replied.

"And did you like the ballroom?"

"But there is no ballroom," she said puzzled.

"Exactly!" he exclaimed and that's just what's wrong with these underpants."

★ ★ ★

As the inspector walked around the bakery he noticed a man pressing down the outsides of the fruit pies with his thumb.

"Hey you," he called, "don't you have a tool for that?"

"Yeah," replied the man, "but I use that for putting holes in the doughnuts."

★ ★ ★

It was Saturday morning and the newspaper deliverer was touring the estate, collecting the week's money. When he got to number 74 Prospect Road he rang the bell but got no answer. Just as he was about to move away, he suddenly had a feeling that someone was standing just behind the door. He put his ear to the wood and could hear a great deal of panting and gasping.

"It's the newspaper man," he called.

A voice was heard from the other side.

"Can you come back in 10 minutes, I'm just in the middle of paying the milk bill."

★ ★ ★

The interview for secretary had been going well until the boss asked

"How good are you on the typewriter?"

"Pretty good," she replied "but I'm better on the floor."

★ ★ ★

A rabbit walked in to the job centre and waited his turn to be interviewed.

"I'm looking for a well paid job," he told the woman behind the counter, "what have you got?"

"Oh my goodness!" she exclaimed, "a talking rabbit."

"Well of course I can talk, what would be the use of me coming in here if I couldn't speak?" he retorted.

The woman thought quickly.

"Leave it with me for a couple of days and I'll see what I can do" she said.

After the rabbit had gone, the woman contacted the television stations and succeeded in getting him a spot on a new talent show that was due to start in the autumn. She couldn't wait to tell him. A couple of days later the rabbit returned and sought out the woman.

"Any luck?" he asked.

"Oh yes," she replied, "I've got you a spot on television..."

But before she could continue, he put up his paw to stop her and said

"That's no good. I'm a car mechanic by trade."

★ ★ ★

Two men were travelling home from work in the rush hour. "Phew, I can't wait to get home," said Colin, "pour myself a double whisky and put my feet up. How about you Dick?" "When I get in, I'm going to tear my wife's bra off." "Really! After all these years, you're still so passionate?" "Oh no, it's not that. It's the straps, they cut into my shoulders so much, especially when it's hot."

★ ★ ★

The town hall was honouring the council's longest serving employee. Bill Treadweaar had cleaned out the men's toilets on Cable Street for more than twenty years and today, he was being presented with a long service award. After the ceremony, he was asked to say a few words.

"Your honour, ladies and gentlemen, thank you very much for this award. I've always enjoyed my job and I hope to go on doing it for many years to come. Mind.... it's not like it used to be. I've seen a lot of changes. Now, kids come down to take drugs, more than they come down to use the facilities – crack, cocaine, there's needles everywhere. Quite frankly, if they do come in for a shit now, it's like a breath of fresh air."

Thank you.

★ ★ ★

"Maurice," said his boss. "Our profits are down so we need to lose some of our workforce, I'll leave it to you to decide who will have to go."

This wasn't something that Maurice was looking forward to, but he had no option. He decided to start in packing. From a distance, he spotted Linda and decided to warn her of what might happen.

"Linda," he said. "I need to lay you or Jack off."

"Well Jack off," she retorted. "I've got a headache."

★ ★ ★

"Doris," said her husband. "I've got the day off so I'm going to spend it in my shed. I don't want disturbing for any reason."

"Okay," replied Doris, knowing how angry he could get if she disobeyed his wishes.

At lunchtime, there was a knock at the door and it was one of her husband's workmates, Jack.

"Is Bob in?" he asked.

"Yes, he's down the shed but he doesn't want to be disturbed," she replied.

He was just about to leave when he turned to her and said "You know Doris, I've always fancied you. How about giving me a quick flash of your tits?"

"Oh no!" she exclaimed, blushing.

"Go on. I'll give you £100."

Doris was strongly tempted. They were desperately short of money and £100 would pay off some of the bills. So she agreed, stripped off her blouse and gave him a quick flash.

"Oh they're beautiful," he whispered. "I'll give you another hundred if you let me fondle them."

So she agreed and later he left, leaving her £200 better off.

That evening at supper she told Bob that Jack had been round looking for him.

"Oh great," said Bob cheering up. "He said he'd pop round to give me that £200 he owed me."

★ ★ ★

A couple moved into a new house, close to a busy main road. Unfortunately, every time a bus trundled by, the wardrobe door would fly open so the woman rang up a local carpenter who came round that afternoon. He inspected it closely but could find nothing wrong.

"I'll just have a look inside," he said, but as he disappeared through the doors, her husband walked into the bedroom.

"What's going on here?" he demanded, opening the wardrobe door.

"You'll never believe this," said the carpenter sheepishly. "I'm waiting for a bus."

★ ★ ★

Jack and his work colleagues were off on their annual sales conference and relaxing in the bar afterwards, they began recounting their most embarrassing moments.

"What about you, Colin? asked Jack.

Colin hesitated and then said "I suppose it was when my mother came unexpectedly into my room and found me playing with myself."

"Well that's nothing to worry about. Young boys often do that sort of thing," said Jack somewhat disappointed.

"Yes, I know," replied Colin, "but this was only last week."

★ ★ ★

A group of men were out on a pheasant shoot when they suddenly came across an extraordinary sight. Scampering through the forest was a beautiful, naked young girl being chased by four men in green uniforms. One of the men was carrying a concrete pole. In a matter of seconds they had disappeared into the undergrowth only to re-emerge ten minutes later.

"Excuse me," shouted one of the shooters. "What's going on?" One of the men stopped to explain.

"We work at the local psychiatric hospital and this is one of our patients. She just loves to escape outdoors and run around naked."

"I see," replied the shooter, "but why is that man carrying a concrete pole?"

"Oh that's his handicap. He caught her yesterday."

★ ★ ★

"So where were you last employed," asked the employment agency interviewer to the out-of-work butler.

"At Lord and Lady Highnose," he replied. "But I got sacked for dropping the soup tureen."

"Mmm, that seems a little harsh."

"It's my own fault, I reacted to their conversation when I should have remained inscrutable."

The butler then recounted the story.

"You see, unknown to me, Lady Highnose had been showing her guest Admiral Reardon, her prize roses and in doing so, he had got a thorn in his finger. Later at lunch, just as I was about to serve the soup, she asked the Admiral how his prick was. It was when he replied that it was still throbbing, that I dropped the soup."

★ ★ ★

Jack went down to the Job Centre and as he was scanning situations vacant, he spotted a card asking for a film scene assistant. The successful candidate would need to have a steady hand to be a bikini line shaver on the latest series of an English version of Bay Watch. Drooling at the very thought, he took the card over to the desk and told the employment officer he was interested in the job.

"Very well," she replied, not batting an eyelid. "You'll need to go to the service station, two miles out of town."

"Really? Is that where they're interviewing?"

"No, that's where the end of the queue is," she replied.

★ ★ ★

Nigel staggered down to breakfast the morning after the office party, with a hangover to beat all others.

"Aagh!" he groaned. "I feel lousy, I can't even remember getting home last night."

"No, I don't expect you would," replied his wife.

"You made a right prat of yourself. First you tried to fondle the boss's wife, then you stripped off and finally you threw a glass of punch in the boss's face."

"Oh shit!" moaned Nigel.

"He fired you," she said.

"Well fuck him," retorted Nigel with a flash of anger.

"I did," replied his wife, calmly. "And he's given you your job back."

★ ★ ★

Maurice had died at the untimely age of 53. He had been a very boring man. All he'd lived for was his work so there wasn't a lot of grief at his funeral. Workmates took up a collection and a headstone was bought with the money. Unfortunately, the stone was erected before the soil had settled and it began to tilt. As a temporary measure, the cemetery attendant wired it up to a nearby tree. Later that week, some of his old friends came to see the finished headstone and one immediately remarked on seeing the wire, "Well bugger me, good old Maurice, still working I see. He's got the phone connected now."

★ ★ ★

Jack was a plumber. He worked for himself and had just finished a job for Mr. Crabtree on Gowan Avenue. As he left, he handed him a bill.

"Prompt payment would be greatly appreciated," he said.

However, a couple of weeks went by without payment, so Jack sent a reminder. Another month went by and still no sign of a cheque, so he sent a second reminder. After another four weeks, he wrote a letter and enclosed a picture of his wife and two children, writing on the back

"This is the reason I need money – to feed my family."

Lo and behold, two days later a letter arrived in the post. It was from Mr. Crabtree. But alas there was no cheque. The envelope contained just one photo. A picture of a voluptuous blonde, wearing a bikini and standing next to a zippy little sports car. On the back of the photo was written

"And this is the reason I can't pay."

★ ★ ★

The tribunal was in session and it was the turn of the defendant to state his case. His legal representative got up to speak.

"Now Mr. Hodges, we have heard that your manner and words to your secretary were so upsetting, she had to take three weeks off work on medical grounds. I wonder if you could give us any mitigating circumstances?"

Hodges got up to speak.

"That morning the alarm failed to go off so I was an hour late getting out of bed. As I jumped up, I saw a note on the pillow from my wife, telling me she'd packed her bags and left with the next door neighbour. I ran down the stairs, tripped over the cat and broke an expensive vase standing on the hallway table. I tried to make myself a cup of coffee but the water had been turned off because of repairs in the street and when I eventually left the house, I noticed the car had a puncture. After another twenty minutes, I set off, only to be caught behind a demonstration march against the building of a new by-pass. So by the time I walked into the office, I was two hours late, having missed an important transatlantic business call, and lost a button off my best suit.

"So," he said, shrugging his shoulders in defeat, "when my secretary cheerfully strolled in and asked me where she should put a new batch of fork handles..."

* * *

The boss called his handsome executive into his office and handed him a bowl.

"Bob, I want you to go next door and masturbate into this bowl."

So the executive, hoping for promotion in the near future, did not question his boss' request but went next door and did as he was asked. A few minutes later he returned and said

"Here it is Mr. Grimes."

"Good. Now here's another bowl. Go and do it again."

So the executive carried out the request for a second time. Over the next hour, the boss told him to do it time and time again until the poor man was so knackered, he begged for a rest.

"Yes, I think that will do fine, Bob. Now you can drive my daughter to the airport, she's got to catch a plane at six."

* * *

"I knew the firm must be in some difficulty," said Gavin to his mate, as they looked at their redundancy notices.

"Really?" replied his mate. "How come?"

"Well they took on my brother-in-law not long ago and he's never worked in a job longer than two months in his life."

* * *

The young girl arrived for an interview to become a trainee executive.

"So Miss Brightly, what are your qualifications?"

"Well I graduated from Oxford with a first class honours degree, having achieved the highest marks ever. I then spent a year in the States, running the day to day business of a small airline and in my spare time wrote a novel on 'modern business practices'."

"Well, that's wonderful," enthused the interview panel. "Is there anything you wish to add?"

"Yes, I'm a pathological liar."

★ ★ ★

After the job interview, the post was given to a voluptuous young girl.

"You'll be expected to do the same things here, as you did in your last job," said her new boss.

"Oh that's fine by me," she replied, "as long as I can kneel on something soft."

★ ★ ★

Lady Mary strolled down the path to where the young gardener was pruning the roses.

"Hello Thomas."

"Good morning Your Ladyship."

"You know Thomas, ever since you've come to work for us, I've been afraid that you would force me to kiss you," she said.

"Oh Your Ladyship, how could I do that with a pair of secateurs in one hand and a bag of clippings in the other?"

"Well," she mused, "you could put the cutters on the bench and rest the clippings against that tree."

★ ★ ★

The young man was selling encyclopaedias from door to door. He had one set left as he knocked at the cottage door and a voice called out

"Hello?"

"I'm selling the latest, most up-to-date encyclopaedias," he called back.

"Okay, can you come round the back," came a voice.

So the man walked around the side of the house, to the back door, where he saw a voluptuous woman wearing a see-through nightie and smiling at him seductively.

"Well, hello," she said sexily.

All of a sudden the man burst into floods of tears.

"What's wrong?" she asked, alarmed at his behaviour.

"I've had a terrible week," he sobbed. "My wife left me on Monday, the house burnt down Tuesday, yesterday someone stole my car and now, today, I'm going to be fucked out of my last set of encyclopaedias."

★ ★ ★

The young girl couldn't believe her luck when her flashy boss took her out to dinner. They wined and dined at the most expensive restaurant in town and then went back to his penthouse apartment. Later, in bed, he turned to her and said

"What would you do if you found you were pregnant?"

"Oh the shame. I could never tell my parents. I'd kill myself," she replied.

"Good girl, that's what I like to hear," he said happily.

★ ★ ★

A rich couple decided to hire a full-time handyman to look after the house, all the outbuildings and also the garden. They offered very low wages so it took a while to select a candidate but out of despair, they eventually chose a man from the neighbouring village. The following weekend they left him in charge while they visited friends in the next county. Alas, when they returned, they discovered the man sitting in their lounge with water pouring through the ceiling. "What the hell's going on?" they demanded. "We hired you to make any necessary repairs. Why haven't you mended the roof?"

"Can't," he replied. "It's raining. It's too wet."

"Well, why didn't you do it while it was dry?" they said in exasperation.

"Couldn't, it wasn't leaking then."

★ ★ ★

"Come in and close the doors," ordered the boss to his young executive. "Now tell me, do you believe in life after death?"

The executive looked puzzled but answered

"Yes, I guess so."

The boss nodded wisely.

"Well that explains why yesterday, after you took the afternoon off for your grandmother's funeral, she stopped by to see you."

365

★ ★ ★

As the factory manager walked into the building, he noticed a youth sitting down on a stool, reading a magazine.

"Hey, you," he called, throwing him £200. "That's a week's wages, pack up and get out immediately... and don't come back."

As the astonished boy left the site, the boss turned to the under manager and said

"How long had that idle kid been working for us?"

"He hadn't," replied his assistant. "He just popped in to deliver lunch from the deli."

★ ★ ★

The down-and-out man had spent his morning begging from street to street. He hadn't done very well and was just about to give up when he noticed a very posh woman walking up the private road to her mansion.

"Excuse me, madam," he said as politely as possible. "Can you spare a bob or two?"

"I'll do better than that," she said. "How are you with a paint brush?"

"Yeah, okay," he replied puzzled.

"Good, there's a can of orange paint here. If you paint the porch round the back, then I'll pay you a decent day's wages."

The tramp disappeared and nothing was seen of him for the next three hours when he reappeared with an empty can.

"All finished?" she asked.

"It is," he replied, "but just one thing," he added helpfully, "it's a Mazaratti round the back, not a Porsche".

★ ★ ★

The man went down the Job Centre and was asked to fill out an employment form. One of the questions said
"Have you ever been arrested?"
The man replied
"No."
The next question read
"Why" (referring back to the previous question if the answer had been yes.)
But the man filled it in anyway.
"Never been caught."

★ ★ ★

A woman moved into a house on a new estate but after spending a week there, she called in the building contractor to complain.
"You never mentioned the busy railway line over there," she said angrily. "Some days it's so bad you can even feel the vibrations lying down in bed.
"Come on," she said, taking him by the arm, "see for yourself."
The contractor lay down on the bed just as the woman's husband walked into the bedroom.
"What the hell's going on here?" he demanded.
The contractor coughed apprehensively and replied
"I know it's hard to believe, but I'm waiting for a train."

★ ★ ★

Three scientists, who'd just been to a meeting on new leading-edge technology in the development of transplants, retired to the hotel bar for a drink. The French scientist began telling his colleagues about his impressive work.

"A few months ago, a man got caught in a garbage disposal machine. All that was left of him was a foot. But we managed to construct a leg onto the foot, then attached the body, other limbs and finally a head and first class brain. Now this man is so efficient, he's found a way of increasing productivity by 50% and cut down the workforce by 100.

"Very good," murmured the other two.

"I, too, have had some excellent results," said the Japanese scientist. "Recently, the eyeball of a man that was blown up by explosives, was brought to our laboratory. We were able to construct a face around this eyeball, then a brain, a torso and limbs. The man is as good as new and, having researched the explosives industry, he has achieved greater safety for all and managed to put 300 people out of work, thus increasing profit margins."

"Very good, very good," reply the other two. Then the English scientist made his contribution.

"Not long ago, we were on our way to work when we passed the smell of a fart. As quick as a flash we caught it in a paper bag and took it back to the laboratory where we constructed an arsehole around it, then a bum, body legs, arms and finally a head. By the time it was finished, the man became the Chancellor of the Exchequer and he's put millions out of work."

★ ★ ★

The young girl was being interviewed for the job of personal assistant. As she looked across the desk at her would-be boss, he suddenly said

"Yes, I think you're exactly what I'm looking for. The pay is £4 above the going rate but that's because I expect my personal assistant to be just that. Very personal, if you get my drift?"

"Oh yes," she replied. "I understand and I'll take the job on those terms."

So, the following Monday morning, the girl arrived bright and early, ready for work. At 9 o'clock, the boss walked in, smiled and said

"Come on Sandra, let's get personal. I feel like a good fuck."

So she left her desk and went into his office where they did the business. Afterwards she remarked

"Gosh, you don't waste much time, do you?"

"That's right girl," he replied. "I also save money. You're fired."

★ ★ ★

The travelling salesman was giving advice to a new employee. "You've got to show you really care about the product you're selling," he said. "For instance I sell ladies stockings and if a woman can't make up her mind I put them on for her."

The new employee grinned knowingly. "Wow, that sounds good."
"Not really," he replied, "my legs are so skinny."

★ ★ ★

A man went into the theatrical outfitters and asked for an RAF uniform, one that Douglas Bader would have worn in the second world war.

"I'm sorry sir, we haven't got an exact match at the moment," said the shop assistant, we've got one from a slightly later era."

"No, no," replied the man. "It has to be absolutely correct. I'm a perfectionist and I'm playing Douglas Bader at the Princes Theatre in six weeks time."

"In that case, sir, if you come back next Monday, I may be able to help you."

"I'm afraid that's no good, I'm having my legs off next Monday," he replied.

★ ★ ★

Dear Marge,
Please help me. My brother is an estate agent and I've just come out of prison for armed robbery. My father spent most of his life in prison as well so my mum committed suicide when she couldn't cope with us and we were sent to a children's home. Now, I have met a wonderful girl, an ex-prostitute, who's going to have my baby. We have a chance to be a real family. Me, Julie, the new baby and her five other

kids. **What I want to know is, should I tell her my brother's
an estate agent?**
Yours worried,
Slasher

★ ★ ★

A young girl had been working at a brush factory for a few
months when the foreman found her in tears one day.
"What's wrong Tracy?" he asked kindly.
"Oh, it's awful," she replied. "I'm growing a brush between
my legs."
The foreman laughed.
"My dear child, that's nothing to worry about. Everyone has that
happen to them. Look..." and with that, he dropped his trousers
and revealed all.
"Aagh," cried the girl even louder. "It's worse than I thought,
you're growing the handle as well."

★ ★ ★

MEET THE WRINKLIES

You know you're getting old when you try to straighten out the wrinkles in your socks and realise you're not wearing any.

★ ★ ★

Three old women were having tea on the lawns of the retirement home and the subject turned to memory.
"I may be 75," said the first old lady, "but I can still remember lying in my cot, just days after being born."
"Oh that's nothing," said the second woman scornfully, "I can remember being born. Horrible it was. Going from a nice warm dark place into blinding light and getting my bum smacked. Aagh!"
Not to be outdone by the other two storytellers, the third woman piped up.
"I'm 86 and I can remember going to Blackpool with my father and coming back with my mother!"

★ ★ ★

Two old ladies chatting in the park.
"I saw Mabel, did you hear old Bill had a massive stroke?"
"He always did Ethel. That's why he was so popular with the ladies."

* * *

Two old men were walking through the park when they came across a girl sunbathing. She was completely nude except for a piece of slate that she'd put over her "triangle" to hide her modesty.

"Well I never!" exclaimed one old man. "How times have changed. Back in my young days, they used to be thatched."

* * *

A simple old woman fell and badly hurt her leg.

"You'll have to rest for a few days," said the doctor, after he'd bandaged it up, "and please don't use the stairs until I give you permission."

The following week, the old woman returned to the surgery for a check-up.

"Very good," said the doctor, "your leg is almost healed. You can start using the stairs again."

"Oh thank goodness for that," she replied happily. "Shinning up the drain pipe was wearing me out."

* * *

A little old lady had reached her 100th birthday. She was still leading an independent life so the local newspaper sent a journalist down to interview her.

"So Maud," began the journalist, "have you been as fit as this all your life?"

"I sure have, young man," she replied, "in fact I've never ever seen a doctor."

"Gosh, that's quite something," remarked the journalist, "do you mean to say that you've never been bed-ridden?"

"Of course I have," she retorted angrily, "and I've been had on the kitchen table but if you print one word of what I've just said, then I'll deny it all."

★ ★ ★

An old spinster was getting married for the first time and the thought of sex was troubling her. When her friend heard about her fears she advised the spinster to get a cucumber and practice with it. The spinster took up the idea and a few weeks passed before they met again.

"Are you more confident about the wedding now?" asked her friend.

"Oh bugger the wedding," came the reply, "I've bought a stock of cucumbers instead!"

★ ★ ★

Two men were returning from the races after losing a packet on the horses. They sat down in a carriage occupied by an old woman and began discussing their bad luck. Eventually, Tom got up and said he'd go along to the buffet car and get them a couple of cans. Bill slumped into the corner and pondered his circumstances.

All of a sudden, the little old lady tapped him on the knee and smiled kindly.

"Come on young man, cheer up. Your good deed will reward you in the end. I think putting your shirt on the horse that fell at the second fence was one of the kindest things you could have done."

★ ★ ★

The old man walked into the surgery and told his doctor he was going to marry a young girl of 21.

"I just want to make sure I'm up to the job," he said, winking slyly.

"Okay," replied the doctor, "we'd better have a look at your sex organs."

The old man immediately held up two fingers and stuck his tongue out.

★ ★ ★

Two old ladies were chatting over a cup of tea in the old people's home.

"It's no good Doris," said one sadly, "Every night I wear my see-through nightie but they're all too old to see through it!"

★ ★ ★

The 85-year-old man went to the doctor's complaining about his love life slowing down.

"When did you first notice this?" asked the doctor.

"Three times last night and twice this morning," he replied.

★ ★ ★

Two old spinsters were catching up on the local gossip.

"I see old Violet Henshaw has just cremated her third husband," said one.

"So I see," replied the other. "Some of us can't get a husband at all, and Violet's got husbands to burn!"

★ ★ ★

The old couple went to Eastbourne for their two week summer holiday but alas, the day before they were due to return, Maurice collapsed and died. He was brought home by special delivery and the funeral took place a few days later. As friends and relatives filed past his coffin, Rose turned to the widow and remarked "Gosh, Ethel, he looks wonderful."

"Oh yes," agreed Ethel, "those two weeks in Eastbourne did him a power of good."

★ ★ ★

Why is an old woman like a turtle in bed?

She moves slowly, is wrinkled, and can't get off her back.

★ ★ ★

An old man had just lost his wife. All he had left was his cat and because he was lonely and had no one to talk to, he thought he would try to teach the cat to talk. He decided to feed his cat the very finest food and then speak to him every day for an hour.

Wonderful salmon, the very best rabbit, an endless variety of birds, this, and much more, was fed to the cat every day. The animal obviously enjoyed the gourmet menu but never said a word. Then one day, the man had just served up a plate of specially prepared mice when the cat shouted

"Look out!"

The old man was so dumbfounded, he just sat there with his mouth open and the next moment the ceiling collapsed on top of him, killing him stone dead.

"Silly bugger," said the cat. "He spends two years trying to get me to talk and then when I do, he takes no bloody notice!"

★ ★ ★

"It's funny how old age affects you," said one old man to the other. "Do you know, it's made my wife's arms shorter."
"Really?"
"Yeah, when we were first married, she could put her arms right round me."

★ ★ ★

The old man was addressing the class of 14-year-olds as part of 'people in the community' week.

"I'm fighting fit," he said. "I've never smoked, I've never had a

drink, I don't eat between meals and I've been faithful to my wife
for fifty years. Tomorrow I'll be celebrating my 80th birthday."
A voice from the back called out
"How?"

★ ★ ★

**One of the problems of getting old is that what should stay
down, comes up, and what should come up, stays down.**

★ ★ ★

An old couple were lying in bed when the woman turned to her
husband and said
"Oh Ben, do you remember when you used to nuzzle my neck?"
"Sure do," he replied.
"Will you do it again, for old times sake?"
"Okay," he said, jumping out of bed.
"But where are you going?" she asked, puzzled.
"To get my teeth," came the reply.

★ ★ ★

**Two old men talking over a pint of beer in the local pub. One
turns to the other sadly and says**
**"You know, George, I'm sick of getting old. I've become so
forgetful. First, I forgot people's names, then their faces...
then I forgot to pull my zip up and now, heaven help me! I
forget to pull it down."**

★ ★ ★

Two old men were sitting on the beach watching the bikini-clad girls walking by, running into the water and playing beach volleyball.

"Do you think all this exercise, keeps you fit?" asked one.

"I should say so," replied the other. "I walk two miles every day just to watch this."

★ ★ ★

A sign of old age is when you wake up to discover your water bed has burst. But then you remember you don't have a water bed!

★ ★ ★

Two old men were sitting in the park talking over past times. They'd got onto the subject of pubs.

"They're more like restaurants, these days," said one.

"And the beer's not so good," replied the other.

"But its the spittoons that I miss," continued the first.

"You always did," came the reply.

★ ★ ★

A vain man was determined to get an all-over suntan, but when he looked in the mirror he saw he was bronzed everywhere except for his penis. Then he had a great idea. He

found a deserted, out-of-the-way part of the beach, buried himself completely in sand apart from his penis which he left sticking out to catch the sun's rays. Later on that afternoon, two old women happened to walk by and one said to the other.

"You know Doris, it's so bloody unfair. When I was eight, I didn't like it, when I was 18, I was very intrigued by it, then when I was 25, I loved it. In my 40's I went looking for it, in my 50's I yearned for it and now in my 70's I've almost forgotten about it. But look Doris, look at that, the bloody things are growing wild now."

★ ★ ★

Two old women limp towards each other along the pavement. As they pass, one points at her foot and says conspiratorially, "Bad arthritis, had it ten years."
The other replied, pointing at her foot, "Dog shit, got it a minute ago round the corner."

★ ★ ★

The delicatessen was the most popular venue in town because the pretty young shop assistant was known to wear no knickers. All day long the men would file in and out, always asking for something on the top shelf so that she had to climb up the ladder and reveal all.
In recent weeks there'd been a box of raisin shortcake on the top shelf and, of course, they'd never been so popular!

Dozens of times a day she'd be up and down the ladder and was just reaching for another tin when an old man came into the shop.

"I suppose yours is raisin too," she called down to him.

As he looked up and saw the delights on offer he replied, "Not yet, but it's beginning to stir."

★ ★ ★

Two blind old ladies walk into the gents toilet by mistake to freshen-up. Two men had also just gone in and on seeing the ladies find themselves in a very embarrassing position. Hoping not to be noticed they stand very still. The first lady mistakes one of them for the washbasin. She grabs hold of his willy, pulls it a couple of times and, unable to stop himself, the man begins to pee.

"At least they have nice warm water in here," she remarks to her friend.

"Well this is even better," replies the second, "it dispenses soap as well."

★ ★ ★

An old man was fed up with the looks his young wife would get from young leering men, so the next time it happened he decided to take revenge.

They happened to go away for the weekend to a country hotel deep in the heart of Sussex. The assistant manager couldn't take his eyes off the beautiful wife as they signed in, so the old man suggested a wager.

"If you can do everything I can do to my wife, then I will pay double for the room."

The assistant manager agreed so the husband kissed his wife on the lips and so did the man. Then he fondled her breasts, as did the man. Finally he put his hand up her skirt and tweaked her backside. The man did likewise.

"Now," said the husband, "watch carefully."

He pulled his todger out of his trousers and bent it in half.

"Okay, okay," said the assistant manager. "You win, the room is free."

★ ★ ★

A very old couple in their 80's went to the doctor for their annual check-up. All seemed well apart from the fact that the wife was worried they were both getting very forgetful.

The doctor replied "If it's worrying you that much, I think I have an idea. Keep a pad and pencil close by and whatever you do, or are planning to do, just write it down on the pad to remind yourselves."

So the couple returned home and later that afternoon, the wife said to her husband

"Jack darling, I fancy a nice cup of tea. Put a slice of lemon with it, please and also bring me a couple of digestive biscuits."

The husband got up to go to the kitchen when she said suddenly "Oh and don't forget to write it down."

Her husband laughed. "Come off it, Doris, I'm not that forgetful that I'd get a cup of tea and a plate of digestives wrong."

He disappeared into the kitchen and it was 20 minutes later before he reappeared with a glass of orange and a lightly boiled egg."

"Oh Donald," she reproached him, "where's the toast soldiers?"

★ ★ ★

Two old men were sitting in the park watching the pretty girls walk by.

"You know Fred, I've been sitting here so long, my bum's fallen asleep."

"Yes I know," said Fred. "I heard it snoring."

★ ★ ★

Two old men were sitting in the park watching the girls walking by in their skimpy outfits.

"By golly, Bernie," said one, "doesn't it make you want to sit them down on your knee and kiss and cuddle them."

"Oh yes," replied the other, "but wasn't there something else we used to do as well?"

★ ★ ★

A very old man would take his daily walk around the garden and that would be the most exercise he could manage before collapsing in his well-worn armchair for the rest of the day. One morning he was halfway round his stroll when he found an old golden idol sticking out of the bushes.

"I say, what have we here," he murmured and to his astonishment the idol spoke back.

"Please help me," it said. "I'm not really an idol, I'm a beautiful young girl but many years ago a spell was put on me and it can only be broken if I have sex with a man."

"Oh no," said the man. "I can't manage that sort of thing anymore."

She begged him again.

"Oh please, please help me. I've been lost in this undergrowth for years it may be such a long time before another man finds me."

The man thought for a moment and then replied, "Okay, I've got an idea. I'll just go and call my son, he's an idle fucking bastard."

★ ★ ★

A little old wizened woman walked into the bikers' bar and made her way across to the man in charge.

"Hey sonny," she said. "I'd like to join your club, it's the Marauders, isn't it?"

"That's right," said the man, amused at her request. "But there are certain rules of entry. Do you have a bike?"

"Sure do," she replied proudly and pointed to a massive machine parked outside the pub.

"Do you smoke?" he continued.

"Yep, three packs a day."

"What about booze?"

"Sure, when I'm not planning on going out, I'll have a bottle of whisky."

The man was very impressed and asked, "Well, have you ever

been picked up by the fuzz?"

"No, but I've been swung round by the nipples a few times,"
she replied.

★ ★ ★

How do men know when they're getting old?
They start having dry dreams and wet farts.

★ ★ ★

The grounds of the old people's home were beautifully laid out
with colourful flower beds, tree-lined avenues and a criss-cross
of paved paths. Now Rose would love to come out in her
wheelchair, hurtle around the paths and try beating her record of
getting round the gardens in less than 30 minutes.

One morning she was careering down the east section when a
man stepped out of the rose bushes and indicated for her to stop.
"Have you got a licence for that?" he demanded.

"Sure have," she replied, delving into her handbag and bringing
out her library ticket.

"You may be pass," he said and on she went.

Coming round the corner by the ornamental pond, another man
stepped out and she had to stop again. "Excuse me madam, do
you have insurance to drive that wheelchair."

"Yes Henry," she replied, and showed him her post office book.

"Very well, continue," he said.

Twenty minutes later, on the final path through the avenue of trees a naked man blocked her path. Not only naked, he sported a huge erection.

"Oh no," sighed Rose, "not the breathalyzer again...."

★ ★ ★

What's the similarity between women and dog turds?
The older they are, the easier they are to pick up.

★ ★ ★

The editor turned to the young journalist with words of advice.

"Remember Jenkins, the story is everything. And the secret is to find a story with a different slant, something not expected."

Later that day Jenkins had arranged to visit one of the city's greatest heroes on his 100th birthday. General St Stevens had fought in some of the most dangerous parts of the world, particularly hand-to-hand fighting in the jungles of East Asia. On the way to the interview, the young journalist remembered what his editor had said and tried to think of some searching questions.

"General," he began. "You are famous for your courage in action, but I wonder if there was any time when you were really frightened?"

After a moment of thought the General replied "Yes, I do remember one occasion. We had been travelling deeper and deeper into the sweltering jungle when out of the blue, a huge rogue elephant appeared from nowhere and began moving towards us. Aaargh! Oh no, I crapped myself."

What a great story, thought the journalist excitedly. "And when was this," he urged, "when did it happen?"

"Just a moment ago when I went aaargh," replied the colonel.

★ ★ ★

Two old blokes were talking.

"Come on Bert, cheer up," said Alfred. "Let's go and have a pint of the dark brew, I hear it puts lead in your pencil."

"No thanks, if it's all the same to you," replied Bert. "I don't have that many women to write to."

★ ★ ★

Gerald returned home from the retirement party his friends had arranged at work and he felt very depressed. Long endless days stretched out before him, nothing to do and no money to spend.

"Come on, cheer up love," greeted his wife. "I've got a surprise for you." She took him by the hand and led him down to the bottom of the garden.

"Look over there," she said, pointing to a luxury apartment block down by the river. "All that is ours."

"What!" he exclaimed. "The whole building? But how, I don't understand."

"Well, do you remember how I used to charge you £50 every time we made love?"

He nodded.

She continued, "I saved up all the money and bought the building for our retirement."

"Oh that's fantastic," he gasped, but then a look of sadness passed over his face.

"Oh Doris, if only I'd known, I would have given you all my business."

★ ★ ★

Three aged women were sitting in the park when they heard the sound of the ice cream van and decided to have a cornet each. They played eeny, meeny, miney mo to see who should go and the task fell to Beryl. She took their money, struggled to her feet and set off. It was more than an hour later when Cath turned to the other woman and commented.

"I don't know where our Beryl's got to, I think the old bugger's run off with the money."

"Don't you bloody start," came Beryl's voice from a few yards behind the bench, "or I won't go at all."

★ ★ ★

It was early days in the marriage and the young farmer and his wife were still in the throes of first passion. One afternoon the man was sitting in the farmyard eating his lunch when a chicken raced by, closely followed by the rooster. The man threw the rooster some crusts and to his surprise it stopped immediately to nibble at them.

Just at that moment, his wife appeared and on seeing this, remarked "Oh Shaun, I hope you never get that hungry!"

★ ★ ★

An old couple went on a touring holiday and to their surprise found themselves back in the area where they'd had their honeymoon.

"Oh look George, do you see that barn over there? Remember we made love behind it, up against that fence."

"Oh yes, Ethel," he said, dreaming of the past. "Come on, let's do it again, for old time's sake."

So the old couple hobbled up to the fence, he dropped his trousers and she took down her knickers. All of a sudden, passion erupted and they began the most athletic sex ever seen. For thirty minutes they rocked up and down at a furious rate, eventually falling on the ground in stunned silence. Now all this activity had been watched by a farmer who had been working inside the barn when they arrived. He was quite overcome by what he had seen and when the couple eventually roused themselves from the ground, he stopped to speak to them.

"I've just got to say that that was the most amazing sexual feat I've ever seen. What amazing stamina, particularly at your age! Would you mind if I asked you what the secret was?"

The old man gasped and replied weakly "There's no secret, forty years ago that bloody fence wasn't electrified."

★ ★ ★